Egyptian Hieroglyphics
David Grant Stewart, Sr.
© 2006-2008

Shortfalls of Egyptology

In their earliest forms, Sumerian, Egyptian, and Phoenician are all the same language, which I will demonstrate in future installments. Yet the modern fields of Egyptian hieroglyphics and Sumerian cuneiform need an overhaul. Here's why:

1. In 1930, L.A. Waddell observed: "Egyptian hieroglyphs are a slightly modified conventional form of the Sumerian diagrammatic picture-writing which came into use during the rule of Menes and the 1st dynasty pharaohs; they have the same phonetic values as their parent picture-signs in the Sumerian." [L.A. Waddell, Egyptian Civilization Its Sumerian Origin And Real Chronology, Luzac & Company, 1930, preface]. Mapping early hieroglyphics back onto Sumerian is essential to restore the correct sounds and meaning to the earliest form of Egyptian. Yet little has been done on this foundational task.

Cyrus Gordon lamented: "… even among the senior citizens of academia it is exceedingly hard to find anyone well-versed in both cuneiform and Egyptian. Since those two fields remain the cornerstones of our topic, the limitation is serious." [*Forgotten Scripts*, Cyrus H. Gordon, 1987, page x.] Sixty-seven years earlier, the noted Egyptologist E.A. Wallis Budge had observed that "the Semitic scholars who have written about it have lacked the Egyptological knowledge necessary....and the Egyptologists, with the exception of the lamented Burchardt, have no adequate knowledge of Semitic languages and literature" (Sir E.A. Wallis Budge, An Egyptian Hieroglyphic Dictionary, Dover reprint, 1978 [original 1920] Vol. I, p. lxv). The German Egyptologist Erman "pointed out in a systematic manner the details of Egyptian grammar that have their counterparts in the Semitic languages" as well as vocabulary (op cit., p. lxvii), although Erman's work was highly incomplete. Budge attempted to further comment on this relationship, although he acknowledges that his own knowledge of the Semitic languages is limited. From Budge's time to Gordon's, few steps had been taken to remedy this deficiency.

As Cyrus Gordon came very close to saying, knowledge of Sumerian (the earliest cuneiform language, non-Semitic) and Akkadian cuneiform (Semitic) are necessary to understand Egyptian, and vice versa. Yet as both Gordon and Budge acknowledged, practically no one in the world is simultaneously skilled in these languages. Knowledge of a great many languages is essential to the restoration of the earliest forms of both Egyptian and Sumerian.

I noted this once again as I was recently perusing an Egyptologist's analysis of Facsimile N° 2. He stated that the four baboons were lifting up their hands basking in the radiance of the sunlight. I have yet to find a single Egyptologist over the last two hundred years who has a clue as to the correct meaning of this hieroglyph. The upraised hands in any hieroglyph, e.g. 𓀠 𓀢 etc., always means some form of the verb "pray." This illustrates the truth of what Cyrus Gordon lamented as a serious limitation, that Sumerologists do not know Egyptian, and Egyptologists do not know Sumerian. This would be perfectly obvious to any Sumerologist (provided of course that he discovered that Sumerian and Egyptian in their earliest forms were the same language, which none of them have), because the Sumerian expression for "pray" is 𒋗 - wouldn't you know it; the second character is not in any of my fonts. Let's see if I can synthesize it: 𒅗 but with the 𒀹 on the other side of the 𐏓, 𒀹𐏓, so that the full expression is roughly 𒋗𒅗, which is pronounced SHU IL and means literally "raising the hands" but means "pray." While on that subject, the root of the Hebrew word for "prayer," פלל is nothing more nor less than a complete sentence in the language of Adam indicating the same thing. Older LDS people will recognize it, but I will say no more about it except to add the historical or etymological observation that all Hebrew letters were originally syllables and each had several sounds and a matrix of meanings.

2. Essentially the whole structure of Egyptology is built upon what the great scholar Cyrus Gordon himself calls the "impoverished Coptic language," which is correct. Scholars simply do not know that the much richer language, Sanskrit, is the direct descendant of ancient Egyptian hieratic, let alone becoming familiar with what it has to contribute. I will prove this assertion with countless worked examples as we go along. The Devanagari script is nothing more or less than hieratic rotated 90° with a line written over it. Sanskrit is the direct descendent and closest language on the earth to ancient Egyptian. Furthermore, knowledge of Arabic is essential to understanding Egyptian hieratic and hieroglyphic. Many of the rules are the same. For example, I could not have discovered the name Japheth unless I had known that the final H in Arabic is identical to TH.

3. Languages change over time. Egyptologists extrapolate the sounds and meanings of hieroglyphs of late Ptolemaic Egyptian onto writings dating nearly 2000 years earlier without accounting for linguistic change. For instance, the quail chick hieroglyph 𓅱 is read by all scholars as having a U or W sound. This is correct for Ptolemaic Egyptian. Yet in earlier times, this hieroglyph had an "M" sound. Many characters originally had a matrix of sounds and meanings, the expression of which depended on grammatical rules. Late Egyptian took only one sound and meaning for each hieroglyph, losing much of the richness and power of the early language. Egyptologists fail to account for the existence of linguistic changes in sound and meaning over time, much less understand what the changes consist of.

In the introduction to his hieroglyphic dictionary, E.A. Wallis Budge noted: "In the transliterations of the Egyptian words in this dictionary, I have followed the order of the letters of the Egyptian words, but I cannot think that these transliterations always represent the true pronunciation of the words" [p.lvii]. He then provides many examples of likely inadequacies in the pronunciation of hieroglyphs based on Coptic equivalents, but does not even attempt to address the much more substantial issue of change in sound and meaning of some hieroglyphs between early hieroglyphic writing (2200 BC) and the late Ptolemaic era (1st century BC).

With the knowledge that the earliest forms of Egyptian and old cuneiform are closely related but that late Egyptian and late Semitic languages bear far less resemblance, can you see the fallacy of failing to account for changes in the pronunciation and meaning of hieroglyphs over a period of two millennia?

4. Lack of original scholarship and attribution. The older Egyptologists, especially E.A. Wallis Budge, were better translators of Egyptian hieroglyphics than any of the academic Egyptologists in the second half of the twentieth century. I have cited Budge's translations and those of more recent, highly respected Egyptologists and followed them by my own translations so that you can judge for yourself (see http://72languages.com/hallofjudgment.php). Later Egyptologists often take earlier ones word for word, perpetuating earlier misidentifications while often failing to translate the original characters for themselves (see "The Four Sons of Horus" and other examples below). Egyptologists often fail to follow their own rules. Cowpathing, or mindless repetition of the pronouncements of predecessors (all the while criticizing the same as obsolete!) is widespread, and unforgivable blunders are perpetuated, as I will demonstrate.

I own several grammars of the Coptic language. One of them is modestly entitled "Sketch of Coptic Grammar" by William B. MacDonald, London, MDCCCLVI. This Scot has produced a fine piece of work. Another book I have has the more pretentious title Grammar of the Coptic Language, by a Mr. Black, 1893. This latter book contains the entire content of the former, word for word without the slightest alteration or attribution. What makes Gardiner "the Dean of Egyptologists" [per Hugh Nibley] is not his great brilliance so much as the fact that he documents practically everything he says. You can trust him, even when he is wrong, at least to be sincere and well-founded in his assertions. Where he errs, so has everyone else.

5. The most comprehensive dictionary ever made of Egyptian hieroglyphics (*Wörterbuch der Ägyptischen Sprache*, by Adolf Erman) is now out of print. This does not speak well of the present state of the field of Egyptology.

6. All Egyptologists and Sumerologists labor under the fundamentally backward assumptions of the religion of Darwinian evolution. They do not find the ancient languages to be highly advanced because they are trained not to expect it, let alone look for it. Coptic has been and extrapolated backwards beyond justification, exactly as Darwin's correct observations as to the Origin of Species have been twisted and pressed into service as the Origin of Genera, quite

contrary to observed fact, science, and reason. They are not quite as bad as the anthropologists who go so far as to define the antiquity of a culture in terms of how primitive it is, an atrocious example of circular reasoning. The discovery that ancient languages are more powerful than the crude modern ones simply does not fit their theory, so they ignore it. Egyptologists believe that ancient language is crude and the Bible is composed of primitive fables, and so the whole world of evidence to the contrary is ignored. Eyewitness accounts have been ignored in favor of conscience-salving theories which have no basis in fact nor reason.

The boring documents - sheep counts and inventories of sacrifices to idols and divinations from animal entrails - are the only things scholars can read correctly. The really interesting scientific and historical records are so poorly translated that they read like fairy tales. There are countless ancient records which reveal a great deal of information which the world has not had for thousands of years because they have not been translated correctly. I have found Joseph's tomb in Egypt, the original Egyptian account of Joseph and Potiphar, the original Sumerian account of Noah building the Ark and the Flood, the original Egyptian account of Joseph interpreting Pharoah's dream, Egyptian records indicating what they did with the Ark after the flood and where it is now, and on, and on, and on. These records are commonly known to all Egyptologists and Sumerologists, yet they do not read them correctly and the rest of the world is left in the dark. There is a whole world full of interesting historical records which document the Holy Scriptures but have never been translated correctly.

Champollion: obsolete or simply forgotten?

Almost all Egyptologists mention Champollion, but given the cowpathing I have seen, I find myself wondering who has actually read his work. It is commonly mentioned that Champollion deciphered hieroglyphs in the 1820s and published his book in 1830. My copy says it was finished (after his decease) by his brother in 1836 but the book itself states that the printing of it was not completed until 1841. Surely someone must have translated Champollion's landmark book into English, but I have not been able to confirm the existence of an English edition in print. The two complaints I have against it are (1) he ought to have given Thomas Young the due credit for convincing him of the 180-degree error of his views prior to Young's discoveries (as Sir Alan Gardiner noted above), and (2) he ought to have transliterated the Coptic he uses to save the reader that trouble. Notwithstanding, I found his book to be perhaps the most interesting of any Egyptian grammar ever written in any language, so it is a great surprise to me that it is not used by anyone today that I am aware of.

As an example of this, I have not seen any Egyptian grammars that do more than mention in passing the color coding of Egyptian hieroglyphs, whereas Champollion does an exhaustive job of it. From Grammaire Egyptienne, ou Principes Généraux de l'écriture sacrée égyptienne appliquée a la représentation de la langue parlée, par Champollion le jeune; publiée sur le manuscrit autographe, par l'ordre de M. Guizot, ministre de l'instruction publique, Paris, typographie de firmin Didot frères, MDCCCXXXVI, pp. 7-8. My translation into English:

"Here are the general notions we have picked up by observation, on the use of colors in hieroglyphic writing. Their application to the sacred characters took place according to two slightly differing systems: according to whether it involved painting or large scale sculptures in public monuments, or even small scale hieroglyphs, which were drawn only as sketches, and with black or red ink, on the sarcophagi, stelae, and other monuments of this lower relief kind. In the first system, applicable only to large scale sculptured characters, it was sought, by flat tints, to recall more nearly the natural color of the objects represented: thus, the characters representing the sky were painted blue (1); the ground in red (2); the moon in yellow (3); the sun in red (4); water in blue (5) or in green (6). The figures of men standing are painted on the large monuments according to rather constant rules: the skin is more or less dark red; the hair is generally blue, and the tunic white, the folds of the drapes being indicated by red lines. Yellow skin is ordinarily given to female figures, and their clothes vary from white, to green, and red. The same rules are followed in the coloring of hieroglyphs drawn small on the stelae, the sarcophagi and coffins; but the clothes are all green. In all cases, if the hieroglyphic signs recall the forms of different members of the human body, they are always painted in a red color, as well as certain members of animals, such as the head of a calf, the thigh of an ox, and the sides of one or the other of these quadrupeds presented as an offering."

He further observed:
"Wood objects are painted yellow."
"Bronze tools are painted green."
"On small monuments the color code is not always strictly observed."
"The color blue is particularly reserved to geometric shapes and to building plans."
[The original blueprints!]
"Pictures of buildings sculpted on a large scale, are almost always of a white color, as if to indicate the pale tint of sandstone and limestone."
"Various colors are given to vases, the series of which is quite numerous among the sacred characters; the different tints indicate the material of each kind of vase."
"Those whose purpose was to contain solid matter, such as bread, meat, fruit, etc., were of terra cotta and are consequently painted red."
"Vases of bronze are painted green; objects of iron are painted red, such as war chariots, sabers, etc."
"Finally, vases of glass, of enamel, or of enameled earthenware, suitable for containing liquids, have their upper part painted blue, the color of the glass or of the enamel, and the lower part of red, to indicate either the liquid or the transparency of the vase."

Champollion observed that this is not a matter of taste in decor, but each color has actual linguistic significance according to a code which is strictly observed in all cases. Champollion also pointed out that all Egyptian hieroglyphs are graphic representations of actual objects existing in nature.

You can consult or download your own copy of Champollion's landmark masterpiece at this website: http://efts.lib.uchicago.edu/cgi-bin/eos/eos_title.pl?callnum=PJ1135.C45 . It is of course in early nineteenth century French.

More Errors in Egyptology

Egyptology seems to have been at its peak at about 1875, as a comparison of historical translations suggests. It is fashionable among Egyptologists to pooh-pooh the work of Sir E. A. Wallis Budge as obsolete, but I have found his translations more accurate and honest than anything done since his time. Errors and absurdities occur repeatedly in the way Egyptian is taught. For example, Gardiner says that the Egyptian word for "thirst" ▽ ≈ is pronounced IB [Egyptian Grammar, Sir Alan Gardiner, editions 1927, 1950, 1957, 1964, 1966, 1969, 1973, Griffith Institute, London. p. 50]. This is a little bit absurd, seeing that the following three wavy line hieroglyph ≈ for "water" is ignored. IB ▽ refers to the heart and actions of the heart - love, wish, desire, want. The correct expression is ▽ ≈ IB-MU, "want-water." That's thirst.

Gardiner also says that the three hieroglyphs for "south wind" should be pronounced "RSW" [op. cit., p. 61] yet this is nothing more than the plural [-W] of "south" [RS].* The hieroglyph for wind is ignored in the transliteration accepted by Egyptologists. Somebody needs to ask, How, then, did the Egyptians distinguish between "south" and "south wind" in the spoken language? It would require incredible sophistry to answer that without admitting that, gee whiz, maybe we ought to pronounce the hieroglyph for "wind" also, just like the one for "water" in "thirst," and the N in SATAN [that is not, and never was, SET or SETH].

*This is by the way the ancestor of the Romance word for south, SUR [Spanish], complete with its alternate dialectical reading in Egyptian, SUL [Portuguese]. RS or Res (south) is the same root that is translated by Budge as Restau in the Book of the Dead and which I have corrected as "the land south" (RES = south, TA or TAU = land).

Gardiner shows the two hieroglyphs for "man" with an unjustified infixed M [op. cit., p.61] and selects the wrong sound for the first hieroglyph, reading as REMETH, "man", what should in fact be read as LUDHI, Mankind, people (see also the discussion of the Egyptian R-L transformation). I have already demonstrated hat this is the ancestor of the Russian, German, and Anglo-Saxon word for people or mankind, with its singular LU being the language of Adam word for person.

The correct reading for Gardiner's "IAH ('yaeh')" [in loc. cit.] is - well, I'll give that later, but it refers to the earth, not the moon, as I will demonstrate.

Joseph in Egypt

Now I'm going to explain a fundamental problem with Egyptology with a very simple example. Here is a color photograph taken inside what every scholar in the world calls the tomb of Zoser (Dzoser, Joser) at Saqqarah on the West Bank of the Nile in Egypt. [*Egypt in Color,* photographed by Roger Wood; text by Margaret S. Drower, McGraw-Hill; text printed by Western Printing Services, Ltd., Bristol, England; color plates (c) Roger Wood, 1964, printed by Carl Schünemann, Germany, p.59. The book is now out of print].

Now look carefully at the hieroglyphs going down each door post of the false door. You should be able to make out these four hieroglyphs repeated in succession going down both sides: ⌐◠ ⊶ ||||

Every Egyptologist in the world will tell you that this is the tomb of King Zoser or Dzoser.

Every Egyptologist in the world will tell you that this tomb is the oldest tomb in Egypt.

Every Egyptologist in the world will tell you that these four hieroglyphs are pronounced NETERIKHEBIT or something close to that.

Every Egyptologist in the world will tell you that this is the "Horus" name of King Zoser.

No Egyptologist will assign any translated meaning to the Horus name. After all, what's in a name? A rose by any other ...

Every Egyptologist in the world will tell you that this pyramid was built in the year 2660 B.C.

All of which tells you precisely nothing.

The first hieroglyph ⌐, which is sometimes called an axe by Egyptologists, can be transliterated NETER [they get that right] but may also be read in the opposite direction, as can many characters. In this sense it carries the idea of saving and is preserved in the German RETTEN, "to save," and Ukrainian ратунек ("ratunek"), salvation.

The second hieroglyph, the mouth ◠, which Egyptologists incorrectly render transliterate as R, is pronounced "PHA" and means "King," just as in the word Pharoah.

The third hieroglyph ⊶, usually represented by a guttural sound, should be transliterated HAMET and means "The land of Ham" or in other words, Egypt.

The fourth hieroglyph, |||| (four vertical lines) which again, no Egyptologist transliterates or translates correctly, is correctly read JOSEPH [Egyptologists read it BIT, BATAU or some variant with those consonants]. This is the same fellow we meet up with in the so-called "Tale of Two Brothers" which is in fact [when translated correctly] the account of Joseph and Potiphar.

The correct translation of the four hieroglyphs is "The King who saved Egypt, Joseph." This is the same Joseph who was sold into Egypt by the Midianites. Notice that Joseph is not called a pharaoh, because as far as the Egyptians were concerned, although he was king, it was not by royal blood as they recognized it, since he was not even of their race, but he was rather what we would call a viceroy.

The tomb was built after all of the great Pyramids.

The tomb was built in the year 1544 B.C.
So what is wrong with Egyptology? Nothing -- as long as you stick with the Ptolemaic period from which it was derived from Coptic.

To read hieroglyphs correctly from the period of this tomb, however, requires a little more homework. In future installments, I will demonstrate the corrections that need to be made and provide worked examples in addition to indicating the etymologies of these corrections throughout the languages of the world.

The earliest "names of pharaohs" in rectangles found in the hieroglyphs such as "Neterkhebit" for "Zoser" are not names at all. They are statements of the most distinguished accomplishments of the king in question, as for "Zoser" [Joseph], "the king who saved Egypt." The four hieroglyphs running down each side of the false door inside Joseph's tomb, which are commonly called his Horus name and merely transliterated with no meaning, each have separate meanings.

The reason why the Egyptian records say the tomb has been vacant for thousands of years should be obvious - Moses brought his coffin out to be buried with his ancestors as he had requested. The reason why the tomb is precisely 110 Egyptian cubits should also be evident: "Joseph said unto his brethren, I die: and God will surely visit you, and bring you out of this land unto the land which he sware to Abraham, to Isaac, and to Jacob. And Joseph took an oath of the children of Israel, saying, God will surely visit you, and ye shall carry up my bones from hence. Joseph died, being an hundred and ten years old: and they embalmed him, and he was put in a coffin in Egypt" (Genesis 50:18-26).

When I was in high school, the pyramid of "Zoser" was claimed to have been built approximately 4000 BC. Now, archaeologists claim that the pyramid was built in approximately 2600 B.C. They have come approximately two-thirds of the way to a correct dating: their beliefs have changed, and mine have not. Some scholars, such as Herman L. Hoeh, have been astute enough to date Zoser and Joseph as contemporaries. The pyramid of Zoser (Joseph) is the only stepped pyramid in Egypt. The Shield of David ("Mogen David") is inscribed in Zoser's tomb, and it is painted blue and white – the state colors of modern Israel.

The discovery of Joseph's tomb at Saqqara also provides a link between the pyramids of the Egypt and those in the New World. The Americas were colonized by descendants of the biblical Joseph (1 Nephi 5:12, 1 Nephi 6:2). It comes as no surprise that the Mesoamerican step pyramids were built by descendants of Joseph.

The Coptic Foundation of Egyptology
Here is the Coptic alphabet and its equivalents that we recognize. These are from Champollion, p.34, except where noted otherwise.

Upper	Lower	Name	Pronunciation	American	Numeral*

case	case			English equivalent	
λ̄	λ	ᾱλφα	Alpha	a	1
B̄	B	B̄ιΔα B̄HΔα	Vida, Beta*	b, v / v between 2 vowels**	2
Γ̄	Γ	Γ̄αΜΜα	Gamma	g, gh	3
Δ̄	Δ	Δ̄λλΔα Δ̄ελτα	Dalda, Delta*	d	4
ε̄	ε	ε̄ι	Ei	e, short a	5
Γ̄	Γ	Γ̄ο	So**	s**	6
Z̄	Z	Z̄ιΔα Z̄HΤα	Zida, Zeta*	z	7
H̄	H	H̄ιΔα □HΤα	Hida Heta**	i, ai, ei	8
ō	σ	ōιΔα ōHΤα	Thida Theta	th	9
ī	ı	ῑαγΔα	Iauda	i	10
κ̄	κ	κ̄αππα	Kabha	k	20
λ̄	λ	λ̄αγλα λ̄αγΔα	Laula Lauda**	l	30
M̄	M̄	M̄ι	Mi	m	40
N̄	N	N̄ι	Ni	n	50
{	[	{ı	Xi	x, ks	60
ō	ο	ō	O	short o	70
Π̄	Π	Π̄ι	Pi	p, b	80
P̄	P	P̄ο	Ro	r	100
Θ̄	Θ	Θ̄ιΜα	Sima	s	200
T̄	T	T̄αγ	Dau Tau*	t, d	300
Ȳ	Y	Ȳε □Y	Ue Hu*	u, i, v	400
Φ̄	Φ	Φ̄ι	Phi	ph	500
2̄	2	2̄ı	Chi	hard ch	600
x̄	x	x̄ı	Epsi, Psi	ps	700

ⲱ̄	ⲱ	ⲱ̄ ⲱ̄ⲩ	O Ou	long o	800
}	]	}ⲉⲓ	Shei	sh	900
ϥ̄	ϥ	ϥ̄ⲉⲓ	Fei	f	90
☐	—	☐ⲉⲓ	Khei	kh	
☐	☐	☐ⲟⲣⲓ	Hori	h	
ⲭ̄	ⲭ	ⲭ̄ⲁⲛⲭⲓⲁ	Janjia Gangia	j, soft ch g except before a vowel*	
ⲥ̄	ⲥ	ⲥ̄ⲓⲙⲁ	S	hard s; gh	
"☐	☐	☐ⲓ ⲧ̄ⲉⲓ	Dei; Ti Tei**	ti di**, th**	

Sketch of Coptic Grammar, William B. MacDonald, London: George Philip & Son, MDCCCLVI, pp. 1-2.
** Occurs only in *A Compendious Grammar of the Egyptian Language as contained in the Coptic and Sahidic Dailetcs with Observations on the Bashmuaic*, Henry Tattam, London, 1830, p.1.

Here we have the very foundation of Egyptology as constructed by scholars. Any mistake here will be felt throughout the entire structure.

The explanation given for the very existence of Coptic is a final severance from the pagan past by the adoption of an expanded Greek alphabet to take the place of hieroglyphs, Phoenician characters, Hieratic, and Demotic, the three successive stages of writing, each farther removed from the original hieroglyphs.

Already you can see fatal flaws. Remember that we documented that the names for the numbers 6 and 7 in early hieroglyphs were PSI and PSA respectively [JS GAEL]? Each of these characters should correspond to a hieroglyph. Where is a hieroglyph that Egyptologists assign a value to of PS? Or for that matter PH?

Where is the hieroglyph that is acknowledged to have the sound T and D? We documented that ⌒ carries both of these sounds, but Egyptologists do not accept that, even though it is a part of their foundation .

Where is the hieroglyph that carries the sounds B and V?

If hieroglyphs carried no vowel sounds, why are vowels represented here?

What hieroglyph represents a KS sound?

Even if hieroglyphs could be found that meet these specifications, the problem remains that they are not the common ones in the view of Egyptologists. The hieroglyphs matching these characters must be the most common ones. In fact, this alphabet must be capable of reproducing ALL sounds in Egyptian.

Notice the TWO DIFFERENT READINGS given to the letter ⲗ - laula and lauda. It is true that The Coptic ⲗ L and ⲗ D look very much alike. But is this taken into account by Egyptologists? I trow not!

Note that in the Coptic version of the Greek LAMDA we find LAUDA instead. I have previously demonstrated that the 𓅱 which all Egyptologists in the world render U or W should be rendered, in the early state of the language, as M. Here at the very foundation of Egyptology we find the point proven with sufficient clarity and certitude. Yet this is utterly ignored by all Egyptologists.

The foundation of Egyptology is shaky indeed. I have not seen any Egyptian grammar - no, not one - which admits the latitude of transliteration required by Coptic. And even when Champollion points out such latitude, such as the R=P=PH equivalence, it is cheerfully ignored by all of his successors!

Note that the number assigned to F is out of sequence. This is because FEI was an afterthought. As I have demonstrated elsewhere, the letter F did not exist in early Egyptian. It fits between PHI and RO in the numerical sequence, once again demonstrating that it was derived from the soft P (PH).

Here's an interesting case of inconsistency because of ignoring foundation information. Everyone knows that the Coptic character ⳡ "shei" representing the sound Sh, comes from the hieroglyph 𓈙 of the same sound. Yet in Budge's dictionary, he has 𓊪𓏭𓅆𓂻 SESHEM as meaning "action" and a lot of other things [p. 698b], yet he has 𓊪𓅆𓈙 SEM = "action, custom(?) and 𓊪𓈙𓅆 SEM = "deed, undertaking" [p. 666b]. Any explanation as to why the 𓈙 is not pronounced is necessarily specious. The reversal of the order of the second and third hieroglyph need not be explained; any Egyptologist knows that character reversal is a common occurrence, although in my observation it is more common for the Egyptologist to reverse the order in his transcription than it is for the Egyptian scribe to reverse characters for esthetic or any other reason. Nor is it of any consequence that my font has rotated the second and fourth hieroglyphs ninety degrees from the way Budge listed them. The real issue here is that all three of these renderings are the same word, of the same meaning, and of the same sound. The 𓈙 must be pronounced when both Coptic and Hieroglyphs demand that it be recognized as such.

Traditional Hieroglyphic Transliterations

Now let us begin the long journey back, starting with the foundation or first milestone, the characters themselves. Here are the common Egyptian hieroglyphs and their transliterations by scholars over the last 170 years. As a rule, no meaning is ascribed to any of these characters by any scholars, except in those few cases where the syllable the character represents also happens to represent a simple word, usually a preposition.

1	2	3	4	5	6	7	8	9	10
	a	a	a	Ꜣ	Ꜣ	Ꜣ,a,e	Ꜣ	Ꜣ	Ꜣ
	a,e,i,o	i	i	y	i	y,i	i̯	i	j
	i,ei,ia,io	i	i				y	y	y
	aa,ou,o	a	a	ꜥ	ꜥ	ꜥ,gh,o	ꜥ	ꜥ	ꜥ
	o	u	u	w	w	w, u	w	w,u	w
		b	b	b	b	b	b	b	b
		p	o	p	p	p	p	p	p
		f	f	f	f	f****	f	f	f
	m	m	m	m	m	m	m	m	m
		n	n	n	n	n	n	n	n
	r	r	r,l	r	r	r	r	t	r
		h	h	h***	h	h	h	h	h
		h	h	ḥ	h	h	ḥ	h	h
		kh	kh	ḫ	h	h	ḫ	h	h
				ẖ	h	h	ẖ	h	h
		s	s	s	s	s	s	s	z
	sh	sh	sh	š	sh	sh	š	sh	sh
		q	q	k.	q	q	k.	k	q
		k	k	k	k	k	k	k	k
		k	g	g	g	g	g	g	g
		t	t	t*	t	t	t	t	y
		th	th	ṯ**	th	th	ṯ	tj	t
	t	d	d	d	d	d	d	d	d
		j	j	ḏ	j	j	ḏ	j	d
	th	khep							
		du							
							pw		

(glyph)	2	3	4	5	6	7	8	9	10
(hieroglyph)							ntr		
(hieroglyph)	a								
(hieroglyph)	o						u		
(hieroglyph)	dua								
(hieroglyph)							is		
(hieroglyph)							iusir		
(hieroglyph)		shu					shu		
(hieroglyph)							tehuti		
(hieroglyph)							tehuti		
(hieroglyph)							inpu		
(hieroglyph)		nef							
(hieroglyph)		af, kheb					bit		

1. Conventional hieroglyph.
2. Grammaire Egyptienne, ou Principes Généraux de l'écriture sacrée égyptienne appliquée a la représentation de la langue parlée, par Champollion le jeune, publiée sur le manuscrit autographe par l'ordre de M. Guizot, ministre de l'instruction publique, Paris, Typographie de Firmin Didot Frères, imprimeurs de l'Institut de France, rue Jacob N° 24, M DCCC XXXVI.
3. An Elementary Grammar of the Ancient Egyptian Language, by P. Le Page Renouf, fifth edition, London: Samuel Bagster and Sons, 1889, p. 1, 75ff.
4. Egyptian Language, Sir E.A. Wallis Budge, 1910, pp. 31-32.
5. Egyptian Hieroglyphic Grammar, Gunther Roeder, 1920, London, p.6.
6. Die Hieroglyphen, von Dr. Adolf Erman, Berlin, 1923, pp. 23-24.
7. Egyptian Hieroglyphic Grammar, S.A.B. Mercer, London, 1926, p.4.
8. Sir Alan Gardiner, Egyptian Grammar, 3rd ed., London, 1957, p.27.
9. How to Read Egyptian Hieroglyphs, Collier and Manley, London, 1998, p.3.
10. Middle Egyptian, James P. Allen, 2000, p. 14.
*Roeder thinks this represents a wall top!
** Roeder calls this tongs. Others call it a tether.
***Roeder calls this a bend. Others say it is a reed windbreak in a field.
****Mercer calls this a snail. Everyone else calls it a horned asp.

Champollion mapped Egyptian hieroglyphs onto Coptic letters and then, having a critical mass, mapped Coptic back onto Egyptian hieroglyphs. All others have built upon this foundation without serious change for the better. I have not as yet studied exhaustively all works on hieroglyphs published since 1836, but everything I have seen so far suggests that no one has really improved on Champollion; they have only made matters worse. The original foundation ought to have included Sanskrit on at least an equal footing with Coptic.

I think Champollion did a magnificent job for what he had to work with. To get an idea of how hard it is to determine the exact sound of a hieroglyph, consider the fact that any hieroglyph may be written with or without phonetic complements or determinatives. Even if you have an idea from Coptic as to how a word should be transliterated, which of the hieroglyphs are determinatives and which are phonetic complements? This can be very difficult to establish because many hieroglyphs can play either role, and which are used is often arbitrary.

Champollion classifies all hieroglyphs into three categories: figurative, tropic, and phonetic. [in loc. cit.] By figurative he seems to mean a figure suggesting the idea intended; tropic, an actual sketch of the object; phonetic, an object carrying the same sound or part of the sound of the word intended. Between these two assumptions, you can see that the door is closed for any character to have any use other than the one prescribed. We'll see him revise this statement later, because for example the hieroglyphs 𓅓 𓈖 𓂋 are recognized by all Egyptologists to have the sounds M, N, and R respectively in all other words, yet still have independent meaning when standing alone, as prepositions, in addition to the fact that any hieroglyph accompanied by a short vertical line is then understood to stand for the object depicted as literal in its own right. For example: 𓂋 stands for the sound R within a word; alone it means locative case as concerns tangible objects; and followed by the short vertical line 𓂋𓏤 it is to be taken literally as "mouth." But by restoring the P sound to 𓂋 it immediately becomes obvious that this locative particle is the ancestor of the Russian locative particle по and the Danish locative particle på, all three pronounced exactly the same way and all three used for exactly the same meaning: 𓊪𓂋𓎛𓏛 𓂋𓏤𓏤𓈖, "Ptah speaks *with respect to* this matter"; Разве Вы говорите по-русски?, "Perchance do you speak [*with respect to, according to the manner of*] Russian?"; De må prøve at svare på spørgsmålene, "You must try to answer *with respect to* the questions."

At the top of page 47, Champollion states that the sounds of the hieroglyphs never seem to have changed at all throughout all Egyptian history: "La valeur individuelle, aussi bien que la forme de chaque signe, ne paraissent point avoir éprouvé d'altération sensible." He adduces no proof for this claim, which I have already demonstrated is false on multiple counts. Champollion's own writings also provide hints that this is not so.

Champollion noted something very interesting that our modern Egyptologists seem to have forgotten if indeed they ever knew: that in the late state of Egyptian, hard and soft sounds were represented indifferently by the same hieroglyphs. Many of the characters have a hard sound and a soft sound. Hebrew also does this, e.g. S=Sh, T=Th, B=Bh (Castillian Spanish B), C = Ch and so on. In early Egyptian, many Hebrew words can be found by simply hardening or softening the consonants. Cf. Hebrew Jasher, Egyptian Yaker, both meaning perfect or upright.

Champollion pointed out that the spelling of Egyptian words varies widely during the Greco-Roman period. This is to be expected because the individual characters lost their meanings and were used only for their sounds at that late stage of degradation, so that any character having the same sound would do.

At the end of Egyptian history of using the hieroglyphs, the only sound variations were according to Egyptian speech at the time. At the beginning of their history, every character not only had multiple sounds, but also had many meanings.

We owe a great debt of gratitude in Egyptology, first of all, to Thomas Young, who enlightened Champollion as to how to go about it.   We owe a great debt of gratitude most especially to Champollion. Everyone who has received any benefit whatsoever from any translation from Egyptian hieroglyphics or hieratic owes a great debt of gratitude to him. No one would have gotten anywhere with out him.

We owe a debt of gratitude to Samuel Birch. He spent countless hours traveling all over Europe copying down Egyptian inscriptions in private collections. He trained himself in Chinese because he knew that much of the logic in Egyptian characters was preserved in Chinese characters. With this knowledge, he compiled a dictionary of Egyptian hieroglyphics into English in the middle of the 19th century.

We owe a debt of gratitude to Sir Ernest A. Wallis Budge. This man translated more hieroglyphic and hieratic records into English than anyone I know, and wrote more books on Egyptology than anyone I know. Practically everything that he translated included a transcription of the original hieroglyphs so that we could check every part of his translations for ourselves. He even wrote several books in simple language on how to learn to read Egyptian hieroglyphic characters and a two volume dictionary of Egyptian hieroglyphs into English, including an English to Egyptian supplement for translating back into Egyptian. The great value of Budge's work is that whether or not you agree with his translations, he has provided you with clear, easily legible copies of the original ancient records for your own use. I know perfectly well what the modern Egyptologists say about him, but in my view, a scholar with the vast experience that he had should not be taken lightly. You may judge for yourself the ethical and intellectual justice in refusing to have anything to do with the very scholar that you quote word for word-- without attribution!

We owe a debt of gratitude to Sir. Alan Gardiner. This man wrote the most comprehensive grammar of the Egyptian language ever written in English and went through three major editions from 1927 to 1957 keeping it updated as much as typesetting expenses would permit with ongoing developments in Egyptology. We owe a debt of gratitude to Adolf Erman -- this man compiled the most comprehensive dictionary of Egyptian hieroglyphs ever written in any language. I am happy to say that I own the works of all of these great men. I have found every one of them to be of tremendous value. It has always been my experience that the founders of any field have had more intelligence and insight than the vast majority of their successors.

Now here's my chart. I will complete it as time permits in the days to come.

Foundation of Egyptian Hieroglyphs by David Grant Stewart, Sr.			
Character	Sounds	Meanings	Examples
𓄿	HAH, AH, A	without	DAH TU HAH DEES, a kingdom below without glory or posterity. The JS GAEL has this phrase in this context, although I alone am responsible for matching the characters with the sounds and meanings. This is the origin of the word Hades which comes to us through the Greeks, but the word is from the language of Adam through Egyptian. These four characters are incorrectly read DUAT by Egyptologists.
𓇋	I	I, me, myself, mine	These characters are incorrectly read INPU by Egyptologists. They should be read MORONI. They are written backwards in deference to the fact that he is from the netherworld.
𓇋𓇋	Y		
⌐◨	OH	blood	This font representation is not quite correct. The correct hieroglyph is the outstretched arm with nothing in the hand and the palm down. These characters are incorrectly read ERPAT by Egyptologists. They should be read PHA RA OH and they mean "king by royal blood" (Abraham 1:20).

𓄿	MO, EM, AM	pluralizing suffix	𓇋𓈖𓊪𓃡𓅓 These characters are incorrectly read INPU by Egyptologists. They should be read MORONI. They are written backwards in deference to the fact that he is from the netherworld. Four more examples from the Paut Khemennu, the "Company of the Eight," said by Egyptologists to be the primeval gods of Egypt: 𓏤𓏤𓃡𓅓 and 𓏤𓏤𓃡𓆑𓅓 Ham and Mrs. Ham, respectively, incorrectly read by all Egyptologists as Hehu and Hehut, which is meaningless. and 𓂝𓂝𓃡𓅓 and 𓂝𓂝𓃡𓆑𓅓 Shem and Mrs. Shem, respectively, incorrectly read by all Egyptologists as Keku and Kekut, which is meaningless.
𓃀	BA		
𓂋	RA	royal	𓂝𓂋𓅓 These characters are incorrectly read ERPAT by Egyptologists. They should be read PHA RA OH and they mean "king by royal blood" (Abraham 1:20).
𓄹	NAH, P/PH		This is the final character in ELKENAH and LIBNAH (Facsimile No. 1), read by all Egyptologists as DUAMUTEF and QEBEKHSENEF respectively according to their own rules, yet for 120 years they have gotten them reversed!
𓅓	M	instrumental case	Identical to the Russian instrumental case, -OM/-EM
𓈖	M, N	water, land; augmentative particle; sign of next degree, hence past, future, comparative	𓈖𓂝 MULEK which occurs in the 5th Dispensation in the Book of the Dead but is read as something entirely different by Egyptologists (see http://72languages.com/hallofjudgment.php)

⬯	P, PH, PHA (hard sound), R (soft sound)	king, council, mouth	⬯▫⬩🐦 These three characters are incorrectly read ERPAT by all Egyptologists. They should be read PHA RA OH and they mean "king by royal blood" ([Abraham 1:20](#)). 🐍⬩⬯ read by Egyptologists as Zoser but the correct reading is JOSEPH. Also, two members of the Paut Khemennu: ▫⬯⌇🐦 and ▫⬯⌇⌐🐦 incorrectly read GEREKH and GEREKHET by Egyptologists. They should be read JAPHETH and Mrs. JAPHETH.
▫	H		
⌇	H, TH		From the Paut Khemennu: ⌇⌇🐦 and ⌇⌇🐦⌐🐦 Ham and Mrs. Ham, respectively, incorrectly read by all Egyptologists as Hehu and Hehut. ▫⬯⌇🐦 and ▫⬯⌇⌐🐦 incorrectly read GEREKH and GEREKHET by Egyptologists. They should be read JAPHETH and Mrs. JAPHETH. The final H equivalency to TH is preserved in modern Arabic.
⊜	KH		
⬤⬯	HAMET	Egypt, the land of Ham	⌐⬯⬤⬯|||| occurs in the ziggurat at Saqqarah. "The king who saved Egypt, Joseph."
⬩⬯	ASH		Occurs in the name of the idolatrous god Korash, incorrectly read IMSET by Egyptologists. See [Facsimile No. 1](#).
⬭	SH,S		
◹	NG, GN	enclosed garden	Ancestor of the Hebrew letter Ayin, which is read GN at the beginning of a word and NG at the end of a word per Rabbi Seixus (see http://72languages.com/hebrew.php)
⬭	KA, SH, EK	change, you, other, different	⬭⬭🐦 and ⬭⬭⌐🐦 Shem and Mrs. Shem, respectively, incorrectly read by all Egyptologists as Keku and Kekut, which is meaningless.
▣	JAH, G		▫⬯⌇🐦 and ▫⬯⌇⌐🐦 incorrectly read GEREKH and GEREKHET by Egyptologists. They should be read JAPHETH and Mrs. JAPHETH.

⌓	DEES, SID, T	seed, grain, bread, land, offspring, glory; female	⌓ 𓆑𓅓 ⌓ DAH TU HAH DEES, a kingdom below without glory or posterity. These four characters are incorrectly read DUAT by Egyptologists.
⇌	TH		
⇌	DAH, Z	provide, protect, possess, hand, kingdom	⌓ 𓆑𓅓 ⌓ DAH TU HAH DEES, a kingdom below without glory or posterity. These four characters are incorrectly read DUAT by Egyptologists.
⌐	JO, Z		
🪲	KEPHER	Adam; generic term for creatures	German Käfer, beetle. Also the origin of KJV "gopher" wood (Genesis 6:14), which is a transliteration, not a translation, of the Egyptian hieroglyph. This hieroglyph occurs on the hieroglyph of Noah's Ark. Adam's body was carried aboard to be reinterred at the location of the crucifixion of the Savior.
◢▭	DA, DI	all forms of the verb "give" including nouns and adjectives	Occurs in the phrase "Adam on di Ahman." This root is preserved in Spanish dar, to give, Rus. дар, gift, дать, to give, and so on.
𓅓	PW, WR, MAL	augmentative (WR); diminutive (PW)	This hieroglyph is the ancestor of English few, French peu, Slavic MAL (small), Romance MAL (bad), and English small. cf. Genesis 47:9, "few and evil have the days of the years of my life been..."
𓊪	NETER, RETTEN	Any form of the verb "save" including nouns and adjectives.	𓊪⌐⇌|||| occurs in the ziggurat at Saqqarah. "The king who saved Egypt, Joseph." This character also appears in the hieroglyph 𓊪 for IUSIR/Jehovah
𓊪	M		
𓈖	MAH MAH	water	𓈖□𓏤 Mahmackrah (Facsimile No. 1), erroneously read as "Hapi" or "Hap" by Egyptologists.

𓂃	TU, O	downward; remote	▭ 𓏏𓄿 ▭ DAH TU HAH DEES, a kingdom below without glory or posterity. These four characters are incorrectly read DUAT by Egyptologists. In a different degree (i.e. later stage), this can refer to the Telestial kingdom (a kingdom – remote in time and space – without posterity). Ancestor of the Greek τηλου, construct form τηλε (tele), remote in time or space. It is the ancestor of the O in our word "other" ["remote" + Anglo-Saxon dual]. Also occurs in the name OMER, remote from the beloved homeland of Egypt (MER = an early name of Egypt).
𓅾	DE (hard sound), J (soft sound)	find	Usually transliterated QEM by Egyptologists. Occurs in 𓅾 ▬ ▭ ▭ Deseret
▬	S	pure water	denotes a rock with water in it, signifying pure water. Sometimes simplified to ▭, above
✲	EL	1. God 2. Star or heavenly body	Occurs in the name of the pagan god ELKENAH (called Duamutef by Egyptologists)
☥	ZI	1. Life 2. Priesthood	
𓊗	ISIS	1. Mother 2. Eve 3. Times and seasons	
𓊽	JEHOVAH	The Appointer of Times and Seasons	

ß	USHU MAAT	1. The foundation of seeing by the light of right. 2. The foundation of seeing by the light of truth. 3. The book seen by 3 witnesses. 4. The book seen by eight witnesses. 5. The sealing power.	This hieroglyph is the ancestor of the Chinese word 书 SHU, book.
	ABRAHAM	Reckoner of the heavens	
	ABRAHAM	Reckoner of the heavens	
	MORONI	The Guardian of sacred records by which the world shall be judged	spelled out as
	NEPHI	The fire of My mouth.	
	DESER-ET, JOSEPH	1. Honeybee. 2. The land of Joseph. 3. The western land. 4. The red land. 5. The Holy land. 6. A land consecrated and set apart from other land masses.	spelled out as (alternate spellings below)

Observations on Champollion

⌒

This is almost too trivial to mention, but I will since I should not take anything for granted. Champollion correctly states that the hieroglyph representing the mouth ⌒ has an R sound. Every Egyptologist knows that it can also represent an L sound (see the Egyptian R-L transformation below). What they do not know is that is also represented in the more ancient records, a PH and P sound, which I explained previously, just as the original Phoenician P had both sounds but the Greeks took it for its R sound and the Romans took it for its P sound. This character ⌒ meant mouth, king, counsel, council, etc. Anciently quorums and councils met around a circular table, which this hieroglyph describes.

Its descendants are Hebrew פה , PEH, mouth; Greek λεγω [λε+εγω] [speak +

I], mouth; Russian рто, rto, mouth; German Rad, counsel and council; German rot = English red; German Reden, to speak; Portuguese falar, Spanish hablar, French parler, Italian parlare, Latin Rex, king; French roi, Spanish rey, and so on.

This same hieroglyph placed at the inside bottom of a circle is called by Egyptologists PAUT and is said to mean a "company." A more accurate translation is "circle of counsel," "cycle," "quorum," all of which mean the same thing. PAUT in hieroglyphs spelled out is, ▯ 𓅱 ⌒ , which is the ancestor of the Latin TEMP (read right to left and accepting the alternate M sound of 𓅱 ⌒ spelled out, as I already demonstrated), Danish TIMER, hours; etc.

⌒

In his excellent chart matching hieroglyphs, hieratic, and Coptic characters [beginning on p. 35, op cit.], Champollion places the hieroglyph ⌒ in the column of those which have the transliteration of Coptic Ϭϭ[S s] and Ⲕк. I have previously demonstrated that ⌒ ⌒ 𓅱 𓆼 should be read SHEM and not KEKU. I should point out that S and SH are the same letter in unpointed Hebrew; that is, the difference is determined only by context. A point in Hebrew has the effect of doubling the consonant, which in that language distinguishes S from SH. And here we have a doubled ⌒ .

✫

Champollion correctly states that the five pointed star hieroglyph ✫ represented a God or divine essence. But it also stood for any heavenly body. This set of meanings is congruent with those of the cuneiform character ➤╪ of the same meaning. Egyptologists generally know this. What they don't know is that the pagan god they call Duamutef should be rendered Elkenah. The first character in the spelling of the name, ✫, should be pronounced EL, not "Dua." The four canopic jar pagan gods represent the four quarters of the earth, as every

Egyptologist knows. Then why do they read as "Duamutef" what should be read as "Elkenah?" "Mutef" is not a place. "Kenah" is. The god of Kenah.

☥

Champollion equates ☥ with ⲁⲁ and ⲱ but it was ZI in the earliest stage of the language. In Linear B the character occurs and is pronounced ZA, which also happens to mean "life" in archaic Greek.

⌐ and ⩞

Champollion equates ⌐ and ⩞ with the Coptic character ⲁ [= a]. If you consult my chart, you will see that the right angle hieroglyph should be transliterated M and the double right angle hieroglyph should be transliterated MM. As the example given there, this hieroglyph occurs most frequently in the name of the pagan god Mahmackrah [see PofGP Facsimile Nº 1, figure 7], erroneously read by Egyptologists as HAP or HAPY because they also read it backwards from what it should be.

On page 46, Champollion states that the compound hieroglyph ⌐⌐ [or ⩞] followed immediately by the hieroglyph 𓀢 has the sound ⲗⲙ or ⲣⲙ [LM or RM]. So what? Well, you remember what the hieroglyph 𓀢 means: pray. And you remember the root of the word pray in Hebrew: פלל [PLL]. And you remember that in
hieroglyphs, R=L [but I also showed you an R=PH equivalence]. So by implication, what is Champollion saying the sound of ⩞ or ⌐⌐ should be? That's right, MM. In fact these mason squares are the very ancestors of our letter M. This character means water. This ⩞ is an Egyptian dual, "the two waters."
The same thing is preserved in Hebrew מימ MAIM, water. In fact Hebrew has no grammatical singular for the word. Why are there two of them? Because there are waters above in the clouds, and there are waters below in the rivers, lakes, and oceans:

> "And God said, Let there be a firmament [עיקר] in the midst of the waters, and let it divide the waters from the waters. And God made the firmament, and divided the waters which [were] under the firmament from the waters which [were] above the firmament: and it was so." (Genesis 1:6)

I need to stop and explain the translation of עיקר ["Raukeeyang"] according to the transliteration system of Joshua Seixas, which is the only correct one I have ever seen. The translation "firmament" for the Hebrew word utterly misleading. Even Luther has "Feste," a solid mass. In the early 19th century, the only correct translation in the world of this word was found in the JS [Joseph Smith, not Joshua Seixas, his Hebrew teacher] translation of the Book of Abraham:

"And the Gods also said: Let there be an expanse in the midst of the waters, and it shall divide the waters from the waters. And the Gods ordered the expanse, so that it divided the waters which were under the expanse from the waters which were above the expanse; and it was so, even as they ordered. And the Gods called the expanse, Heaven. And it came to pass that it was from evening until morning that they called night; and it came to pass that it was from morning until evening that they called day; and this was the second time that they called night and day" (Abraham 4:6-8).

The meaning of the word the *expansion that is* produced in matter by some process. For example, if you beat a sheet of gold into a thin foil, you have produced a עיקר in the surface area of the gold. If you add baking soda to vinegar, you produce and immediate עיקר in its volume. The action of yeast upon bread dough produces a עיקר, in a few hours in the volume of the dough. If you light a firecracker, in a few milliseconds after the fuse burns down, you will have a great עיקר in its volume, accompanied by enough noise to get your attention.

The *result* of this עיקר was what the Anglo-Saxons called heofon [= heaven], cognate with heave, something thrown upward. We would translate the word Heaven as used in Abraham 4:8 above as *atmosphere.* To demonstrate that this is how it is used in that verse, consider a later verse in the same book:

"And the Gods said: Let us prepare the waters to bring forth abundantly the moving creatures that have life; and the fowl, that they may fly above the earth in the open expanse of heaven" (Abraham 4:20)

Obviously, the part of the atmosphere called the troposphere is what is meant.

Now back to the abbreviated water hieroglyph. I say abbreviated, because ⌐⌐ and ⩘ are very short forms of 〜 and 〰 which are in turn short forms of the most common expression for water ☰, just as N was originally a short form of M.

The most common place I have seen the hieroglyph ⩘ is in the name of the pagan god ⩘□⫯ which as you already know, every Egyptologist transliterates as HAP or HAPY and translates as "the god of the Nile" but you know should be transliterated as MAHMACKRAH and translated "the god of the waters." The Egyptologists may be excused for calling it the god of the Nile, although not lexically correct, the logic is not entirely defective [except for the duality of the hieroglyph]. It does not rain in Egypt, any more than it snows in Los Angeles.

Now you can see that ⌐⌐⫯ or ⩘⫯ means praying to the pagan god

Mahmackrah, the god of the waters, presumably so that the Nile will not rise too high and cause a flood, nor too low and cause a famine.   This hieroglyph serves an unwitting purpose to me. If I see it in any document, I will likely not bother to translate it. It probably will not contain any useful information. Unless of course the document is written by some enlightened person who is merely mentioning in passing, the native customs of the time.

ſ

On page 49, Champollion has the word for year, ſ pronounced ρoⲙⲡⲉ, ROMPE, [also means grass or perennial herbs covering the ground] which is interesting because it is closer to modern Malay RUMPUT, grass or perennial herbs covering the ground, than the present-day Egyptology rendering of RENPET for the same thing. RENPET literally means "the name of heaven" which Champollion would not have recognized with his ρoⲙⲡⲉ, ROMPE, year, but ρⲁⲛ, RAN, name. His logic for ſ meaning "year" was that "un rameau de palmier ſ représentait l'année, parce qu'on supposait que cet arbre poussait douze rameaux par an, un dans chaque mois," "a palm tree branch [frond] ſ represented the year, because it was supposed that this tree put forth twelve branches a year, one in each month." [p. 24]. I think such efforts are commendable, because even if they are not correct, they can still be good mnemonics. I think he is quite right in this case.

⌐⌐⌐

He has ⌐⌐⌐, a broad necklace, meaning gold, pronounced ⲛoⲩⲃ NOUB, which is the origin of the name of the land of NUBIA.

My fonts don't have it, but the next character is composed of three hieroglyphs superimposed: the vaulted sky ⌐ with the dark cloth ǀ veil of night drawn over it, from which a star ⋆ is suspended. This is night, as he says it is. He says the pronunciation is ϣⲱⲣ/ SORH which is at odds with modern scholars' GEREKH but it is interesting in that ϣⲱⲣ/   is almost identical in pronunciation to the French word of the same meaning, "soir."

At this point, Champollion inserts as an illustration, a simplified hieroglyphic account of the Bar of Judgment which has all the basic elements. It has very little running text, and the defendant is shown with his hands raised toward heaven in prayer, and he is flanked by female figures representing right and truth (see http://72languages.com/hallofjudgment.php)

🚶 and 🚶

It is curious that Champollion assigns sounds for man and woman, 🚶 and 🚶 as ρⲱⲙⲉ and /ⲓⲙⲉ, ROMEH and HIME, very close to his own native French, HOMME and FEMME respectively. Modern Egyptologists sound them IS AND

ISET but the hieroglyphs they use should be transliterated ISH and ISHAH respectively, because the final T or TH in Egyptian is identical to the final H just as it is in Arabic: مِشأ ISHAH but مِشَةأ ISHAT - you see they are identical except for the two dots at the upper left, or end, of the word. But classical Arabic was not pointed. Modern Arabic uses different words, but ISH and ISHAH are identical to the classical Hebrew words for man and woman, איש and אישה respectively. The full Egyptian expressions are ⌐°— 𓀀 and ⌐°—◠𓀀. The ⌐°— represents an SH sound as it does in the name of the pagan god KORASH. The second hieroglyph in the case of the woman, ◠, is the sign of the feminine, but it is also exactly the same letter in hieroglyphic as the ة was in Arabic and follows exactly the same rules - it may be T, TH, or H, according to context. ة is the stand-alone form of the same letter that looks like a little wave at the end [left side!] of the word مِشأ. And I don't suppose you failed to notice that the ة even slightly resembles its hieroglyphic ancestor ◠.

Example Phrases

⊙◠𓏭◠⌐°—𓀀◠.

⊙◠. ANOKI, I [am]. These two hieroglyphs occur at the 9:00 position of Facsimile Nº2, outer ring.

𓏭◠⌐°—𓀀. ITFI. Egyptologists do not pronounce the FI. Father. If the Egyptians wrote this backwards as a sign of respect, as they do in many cases, this FATI, father, would be an exact analog to MUTI, mother.

◠. K, EK, KA, etc. 2nd person personal pronoun, thou, thee, thy.

⊙◠𓏭◠⌐°—𓀀◠. ANOKI FATIKA. I am thy father.

〰◠◠𓊃𓏭𓏭.

〰◠◠. ANTEK thou

𓊃𓏭𓏭. SI who?

〰◠◠𓊃𓏭𓏭. ANTEK SI? Who [art] thou?

▯◠◠𓀀◠〰◠. PETRY RENKA? What is thy name? Interrogations like this occur a great deal in the Book of the Dead, where the deceased has to provide the names of the sentinels in order to pass by them. The purpose of the endowment was to provide these names.

𓏲◠〰𓀀𓅃𓏺.

𓏲◠. JED, originally RZHED, ancestor of German REDEN, to speak, discuss.

〰. N, sign of degrees. This shifts the verb to the second degree, corresponding to our past tense.

🦅. I, meaning, I.

🦅. M, sign of instrumental case, same as in Russian, e.g. идти пешом, to go by foot.

ƒ. Called SHU or MAAT by Egyptologists. Originally THUM, as in URIM and THUMMIM, Lights and Truths.

🦅〰🦅🦅ƒ. RZHEDANI MA THUM, I have spoken the truth. Said by the defendant before the Bar of Judgment.

🦅🦅🦅🦅🦅🦅🦅🦅🦅🦅. This is the Egyptian equivalent of the Roman QVOVADIS.

🦅🦅🦅🦅. SHEMEK, Thou art.

🦅🦅🦅🦅. IREFHER, upon it.

🦅. SI what.

🦅🦅🦅🦅. ODOS, ancestor of the Greek όδος, road.

🦅🦅🦅🦅🦅🦅🦅🦅🦅🦅. Whither goest thou? [Lit., on what road goest thou upon it?]

Here are some simple sentences from a little book called "Hieroglyphs for Everyone." The analysis is my own, and I have transliterated and translated differently as appropriate.

🦅〰🦅🦅🦅🦅🦅🦅🦅🦅

🦅〰 ANKH life
🦅 EK thy
🦅🦅🦅 IREF will be
🦅 EM in, upon

🦅🦅🦅🦅 ISHESET what

🦅〰🦅🦅🦅🦅🦅🦅🦅🦅
What wilt thou live on?

🦅🦅🦅🦅🦅🦅🦅🦅🦅🦅🦅
🦅🦅🦅🦅 WEDI I put, place
🦅🦅 SU it
🦅🦅🦅 IREF will be

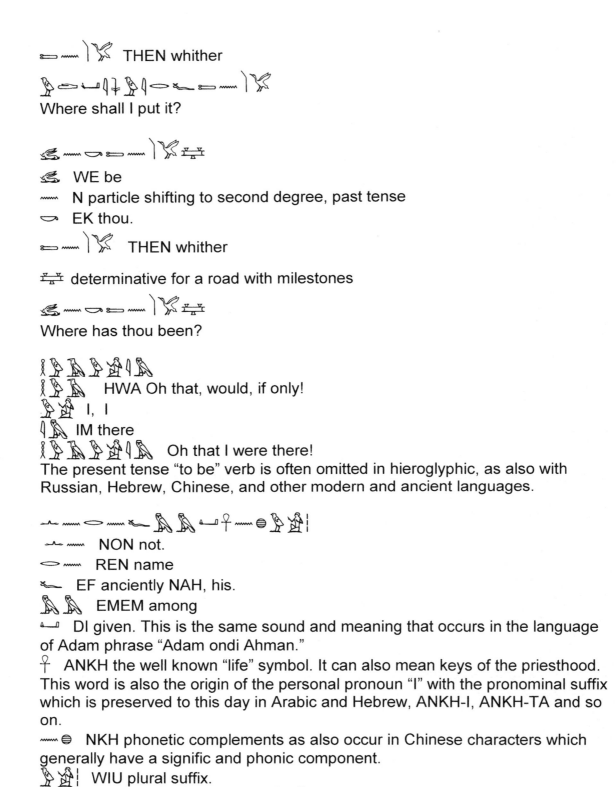

THEN whither

Where shall I put it?

WE be

N particle shifting to second degree, past tense

EK thou.

THEN whither

determinative for a road with milestones

Where has thou been?

HWA Oh that, would, if only!

I, I

IM there

Oh that I were there!

The present tense "to be" verb is often omitted in hieroglyphic, as also with Russian, Hebrew, Chinese, and other modern and ancient languages.

NON not.

REN name

EF anciently NAH, his.

EMEM among

DI given. This is the same sound and meaning that occurs in the language of Adam phrase "Adam ondi Ahman."

ANKH the well known "life" symbol. It can also mean keys of the priesthood. This word is also the origin of the personal pronoun "I" with the pronominal suffix which is preserved to this day in Arabic and Hebrew, ANKH-I, ANKH-TA and so on.

NKH phonetic complements as also occur in Chinese characters which generally have a signific and phonic component.

WIU plural suffix.

His name is not/shall not be among the living. Tense according to context; it is not expressed here.

WOBEN RA EM PET.
The sun rises in the sky.
Very common phase near the head of religious texts.

ANTENU NI IM SU
As for the vessels, they are mine.

SEN sibling
N phonetic complement.
T feminine suffix, preserved as -ETTE and -ESSE in French.
Ideographic determinative for female humans.
JED speak, say
T feminine suffix
NA to. Preserved in Russian на and in Portuguese "na" with the same meaning.

SEN sibling
N phonetic complement.
I ideogram for male, person, me, my, etc.
S grammatical feminine suffix, she, her.

A sister is talking to her brother.

Today I expect to take you through an entire grammar, called "Hieroglyphs for Everyone." Even at this early stage, some of the sentences are taken directly from ancient records, which you will recognize when you see them again. I'll be making many grammatical explanations that aren't in the book.

WEN   be

〰 N   Said by Egyptologists to be a phonetic complement. I say in this case that it is a sign of shifting degree. The first degree is the present tense. The second degree is the past tense. The third degree is the future tense. The verb alone is in the first degree and therefore present tense. This shifts it to the second.

〰   N again. This shifts the verb to the third degree, future tense.

⌒ 𓅂 𓏭 TAY this, feminine.

𓀀 I - I, me, my.

𓎱 HEMET wife.

⌒ T, a seed and a loaf of bread. Also meant land in early Egyptian. Was originally pronounced both T and D. Ancestor of our D. In this case may be considered either as a phonetic complement to the preceding hieroglyph or as a feminine suffix. It is in fact redundant in either case.

𓀗 A ideogram indicating that what preceded refers to a woman.

𓇋 𓅂 IM there, in that place. Ancestor of the Hebrew word שם of the same meaning.

Be - future this female - my - wife - there.
My wife will be there.

UBEN rise. Cognate with German OBEN, above.

⊙ RA the sun.

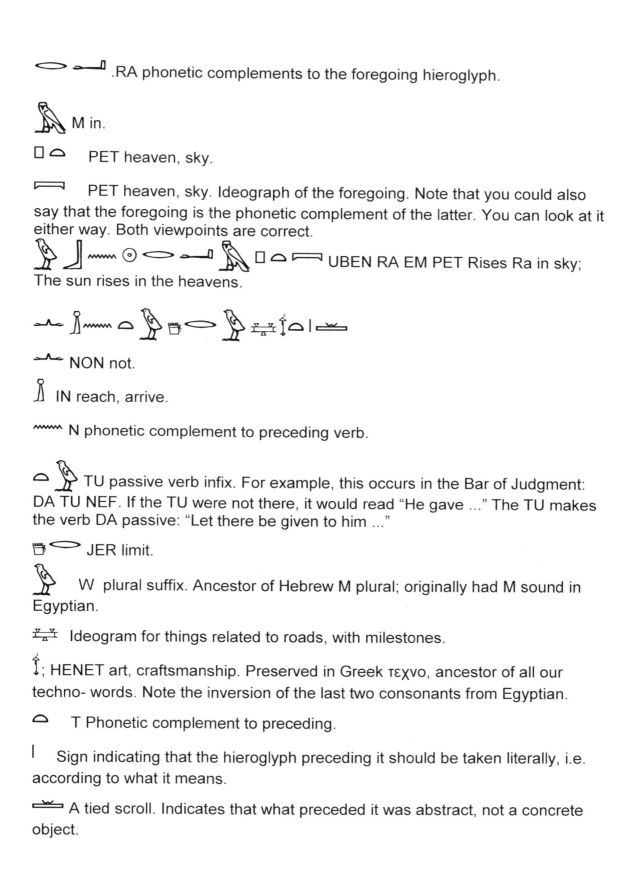

⬭ ▬◀ .RA phonetic complements to the foregoing hieroglyph.

𓅓 M in.

□ ⌂ PET heaven, sky.

▭ PET heaven, sky. Ideograph of the foregoing. Note that you could also say that the foregoing is the phonetic complement of the latter. You can look at it either way. Both viewpoints are correct.

𓄿 ⌐ ∿ ⊙ ⬭ ▬◀ 𓅓 □ ⌂ ▭ UBEN RA EM PET Rises Ra in sky; The sun rises in the heavens.

⌁ 𓃀 ∿ ⌂ 𓅓 ▯ ⬭ 𓅓 ⊹ 𓅱 ⌂ | ▱

⌁ NON not.

𓃀 IN reach, arrive.

∿ N phonetic complement to preceding verb.

⌂ 𓅱 TU passive verb infix. For example, this occurs in the Bar of Judgment: DA TU NEF. If the TU were not there, it would read "He gave ..." The TU makes the verb DA passive: "Let there be given to him ..."

▯ ⬭ JER limit.

𓅱 W plural suffix. Ancestor of Hebrew M plural; originally had M sound in Egyptian.

⊹ Ideogram for things related to roads, with milestones.

𓅱; HENET art, craftsmanship. Preserved in Greek τεχνο, ancestor of all our techno- words. Note the inversion of the last two consonants from Egyptian.

⌂ T Phonetic complement to preceding.

| Sign indicating that the hieroglyph preceding it should be taken literally, i.e. according to what it means.

▱ A tied scroll. Indicates that what preceded it was abstract, not a concrete object.

NON INTU JERU HENET Not reach - passive - limits, art. The limit of art can not be reached.

.MEI not. Preserved in Chinese 没 MEI not.

. PEH attack

. PEH   ideogram for attack.

. ideogram for verbs of traveling on foot.

. ANTY   that which, he who, etc.

. NON not.

. PEH attack.

. EN shifts verb to 2nd degree, past tense.

. EF, he, him. Anciently pronounced NAH.

. MEI PEH ENTY NON PEHENEF. Do not attack him who has not attacked.

2800. Pronouns and pronominal suffixes:

. I, I, me, my.

. EK, KA thee, thou, thy

TH thee, thou, thy, feminine.

. EF he, him, his. Anciently pronounced NAH.

. NU, we, us, our. Same as Hebrew.

. SHUNU, they, them, their. Same as Assyrian cuneiform.

Now more of my observations on Egyptian language and grammar.

Egyptian R-L Transformation

For the Egyptians, R and L were the same letter. Note in the table above that Budge assigns both the R and L sounds to the mouth hieroglyph ⬭ . Many words pronounced with an "L" in Akkadian or Sumerian are pronounced with an "R" in Egyptian. This same dialectical trend is seen in major East Asian languages today. Japanese and some other languages today do not have separate sounds for R and L. The Wikipedia (see Engrish" in the Wikipedia at http://en.wikipedia.org/wiki/Engrish) observes: "native Japanese speakers not fluent in English often mispronounce English words containing the letter L...Korean has no final R sound, and speakers would pronounce it as an L." Chinese has no final L sound and speakers typically pronounce it as R.

A similar Iberian R-L dialectical equivalency is seen with Spanish and Portuguese. Spanish: obligar. Portuguese: obrigar. Spanish: plazo. Portuguese: prazo. Spanish: plata. Portuguese: prata. Spanish: placer. Portuguese: prazer. Sometimes the roles are reversed. Compare Spanish SUR with Portuguese SUL, which is also the alternate dialectical reading in Egyptian, all for representing the direction south. We also see the R-L transformation in words like Latin peregrini and Italian pellegrini, both meaning pilgrim.

The Egyptian word for "child" CHRD is the same as ours, allowing for the R-L transformation - CHILD. No kidding. Compare also Gaelic "la" and Egyptian "ra" = day, light.

Because of the Hebrew sojourn in Egypt during the captivity, the R-L transformation is also seen in some Hebrew words. Akkadian 𒇽 = LU meaning "person" or "people" is composed of 𒆪 KU, garment, and 𒁹 creature, person, individual. Akkadian ALU = city, or "many people." In Hebrew, this becomes Jeru or Iru, as in Jerusalem.

Akkadian cuneiform 𒀭𒇽 God (which I have demonstrated should be pronounced ALE) is represented in hieroglyphic writing by is ⊙ which has the same pronunciation and meaning (although the Egyptians later pronounced it RA – remember the Egyptian R-L transformation as well as the option of reversing text) and has the descriptive meaning of "Man of Counsel," the circle representing the round table around which the counselors sat.

Compare Egyptian APEDU, birds, where you have a root PD or PT, with the Russian птица and the Greek πτερυξ (actually wing), then taking into account the well-known Greek dialectical T-S shift (θαλαττα-θαλασσα) we come down to the Portuguese passaro and Spanish pajaro and finally the digamma ancestor of English F along with the Egyptian and Iberian R-L equivalency and get our own "fowl". The original root here, APT, combines two roots, the first meaning creature A and the second meaning of the sky PT as is obvious to any Egyptologist. For the Egyptian hieroglyphs see Gardiner [op. cit.], p. 60.

Dual Nouns

Gardiner mentions that the word for night has the form of a dual in Egyptian, yet he cannot see why it should be a dual [ibid]. Just as the concept of brother in English is a dual both logically and grammatically, the concept of night has no meaning without its counterpart of day.

Gardiner mentions that the hieroglyph for the forepart of a lion was in its early form a dual but ventures no explanation as to why and offers PHTY strength as its transliteration and translation [op. cit., p. 60]. I explained in an earlier installment that it should be translated "mind and strength" [Bar of Judgment, first section] which explains why it is a dual.

Ditto HNTY "end of a time period" - you can see why the "end of a time period" is a logical dual. Cf. Ecclesiastes 7:8.

Direction of Writing

Most modern languages are written left to right, while Hebrew and Arabic are written right to left. The original language had both possibilities. In Egyptian and other early languages, it was common practice to write a characters or concepts of special significance in the opposite direction as a way of doing the equivalent of what we call capitalization for proper names.

Every Egyptologist knows that that hieroglyph trio rendered by Gardiner Gardiner's "NIWT (NEYWET)" means "town" but what they don't know is that it was reversed and pronounced by the ancient Egyptians as- "TOWN."

Observations on Vocabulary and Grammar

The older forms of Egyptian, Sumerian, and their parent language all had multiple sounds for each hieroglyph, and multiple meanings for each sound. Watch what happens when we restore the original sounds to Egyptian hieroglyphic HRW-RA which Egyptologists will tell you is the Egyptian word for "day, daytime" [Gardiner, op. cit., p. 37], although the Egyptologists always forget that the RA sign should also be pronounced. We get, character for character, εφημερα the Greek word of exactly the same meaning. My, my. What a coincidence. This demonstrates once again (we could do it with every word in the language) that when the original sounds and meanings are restored to each character, we have the keys to every descendent language in the world.

The two Chinese characters ⊣ SHANG "above" and ⊢ HSIA "below" form the character ⊞ WANG, "king." The two Egyptian characters [I don't have the character; rotate "(" 90° clockwise] "above" and ")" [rotate it 90° clockwise] "below" form the character ⌣ PHA, "king," one having universal dominion.

The greeting of a guest in an ancient Egyptian home was identical in meaning to the greeting of a guest in a modern Chinese home-- Egyptian: 𓇋𓏏𓇋, ITI, Chinese 你来了, NI LAI LE, and in sound to the Russian "to go," идти, ITI. The Egyptian and Chinese are both idiomatic expressions meaning "Welcome!" but both mean literally, "You have come!"

Perhaps it shouldn't, but it always astounds me when a word survives four thousand years without significant change in sound or meaning. Such a word is found in Malay "rumput" which is identical in sound and meaning to the ancient Egyptian word for grass or perennial herbs.

An example of a word handed down to us without alteration is the Egyptian word KAW [=oxen], cf. German Kuh, English "cow."

Our word DOWN comes directly from ancient Egyptian with the slightest variation in sound and none in meaning.

The Egyptian word for foot, read by Egyptologists as RED should in fact be read PED and in fact has come down to us through Greco-Roman times without alteration.

The same P-R hieroglyph occurs in the language of Adam word JARED showing that the alternate reading of the hieroglyph was also correct. The word means descendant, that which comes down, and is also the origin of the name of the Jordan River, the N being a geographical suffix, just as GERSHON, "a strange/foreign land" comes from GEREKH, stranger, foreigner, and an alternate reading of Japheth as I will demonstrate below (see Paut Khemenu).

The word MI in Egyptian [Gardiner, op. cit., p. 48] has the same sound and meaning in Sumerian and has the same sound an meaning in the language of Adam - "like, similar." In the language of Adam, we have MI = like, CHA = unto, EL = God. Michael.

The term "magics" does not exist in the English language; however, it is used in the Book of Mormon (Mormon 1:19). It does in fact exist in the Egyptian writing system in which it was written: HEKA, magic; HEKAU, magics [cf. Gardiner, op. cit., p. 59]. Cf. German Hexe, witch.

Gen. 47:9 "... few and evil have been the days of the years of my life ..." The first three words are a single Egyptian hieroglyph, the well-known sparrow, PW, the ancestor of the English word few, French peu, as well as, with the transformations already mentioned, the Slavic "mal" and Latin "mal" and English "small." This is one of many indications that, no surprise, Moses translated his record into Hebrew from original accounts written in Egyptian hieroglyphics.

Russian uses the M of predication exactly the way Egyptian does. The Russian does not say, "When I was a little boy" but rather "When I was as a little boy" Когда я был маленким мальчиком exactly as in Egyptian. The M of predication is the Eastern equivalent of the SER-ESTAR of the Romance languages - two different be-verbs, one denoting an inherent trait and the other an acquired one.

The hieroglyph which is pronounced PR or PER by Egyptologists, was originally pronounced BETH, as evidenced by the phonetic compliments which usually accompany it in early Egyptian, 𓉿◠ .

The Hebrew letter א does not come from the Phoenician letter Aleph 𐤀 as is commonly supposed, but is in fact a representation of the hieroglyph , a bird in flight. In the language of Adam and in old Egyptian, it is the number 1,000 [see Pearl of Great Price <u>Facsimile Nº 2</u>, figure 4: "a numerical figure, in Egyptian signifying one thousand"]. Do you know what ALEPH means in Hebrew? The number 1,000. It also means "expanse" as in the Book of Abraham, facsimile #2, figure 4. Note that the bird there is a different species. There is some insight to be cleaned here.

In old Egyptian, any bird, regardless of species, with its wings outstretched in opposite directions means "1,000." It is exactly analogous to the upraised hands of person or forepaws of an animal or forelegs of flying creature always meaning "prayer" as I explained previously. The position or attitude of the character always has hieroglyphic significance independent of the character represented. This is well illustrated in the Book of Abraham, Facsimile number 1, where the upraised hands signify prayer; they were not really upraised; he was tied down on the altar and his hands and arms were immobilized. This is why Abraham takes care to explain that these are hieroglyphs, not an artistic sketch. The same is true of the position of the legs, being spread apart, signifying fleeing from the scene.

Arabic and Egyptian

I have previously documented that the Arabic script is a descendant of Egyptian hieratic (see http://72languages.com/hieratic.pdf). Here are three Arabic letters ب ت ث which all look exactly alike. Anciently they stood for the hieroglyph which was pronounced BET(H). Today, each of them takes only one of those sounds, B, T, and TH respectively, going right to left as the characters are written. The dots distinguish them today.

Here are three more Arabic letters which are exactly alike, again distinguished only by dots: ج ح خ . They are today pronounced J, H, and KH respectively. The ancient Egyptian hieroglyph they stand for 𓊖 could assume all of these sounds.

This is the same ⬛ we find in ⬛ ⬡ 𓂗 which scholars incorrectly read GEREKH. It should be read JAPHETH, and now you know why.

The Arabic letters ع غ likewise stood for the two sounds of the Hebrew ע. The Hebrews have, with the exception of Rabbi Joshua Seixas, forgotten all its sounds, which were originally GN, NG, and O. The Arabs preserve the two sounds and distinguish them today with a dot for the hard sound.

The Arabic letters ف ق which are identical in flowing text, originally represented the hieroglyph 𓂧 and was pronounced COPH and could represent either C or PH or both sounds. Now they are two separate letters distinguished by one or two dots.

The Arabic letters ر ز R and Z respectively, reading right to left, anciently represented the sound RZH which is preserved in Polish and Czech to this day.

The Arabic letters ط ظ originally represented an Egyptian hieroglyph that stood for the sounds TS and DZ respectively, reading from right to left, and are now separated into two separate characters distinguished only by a dot.

I mention these observations because they establish the fact that the ancient language was iterative, i.e. every character had several sounds and several meanings which are well documented for example in Sumerian cuneiform but were used simultaneously as scholars do not generally recognize but admit in some cases such as the obvious case of 𓆃 representing Right and Truth. Without a knowledge of all these principles, ancient Egyptian cannot be translated correctly except in the crude, late, Ptolemaic forms.

Egyptian Hieroglyphs: Alphabetic or Syllabic?

I want to take you through an old Egyptian grammar written in 1874 by a French scholar, P. le Page Renouf. It is of unusual interest because the man does his own thinking, a refreshing departure from the cowpathing of the 133 years since. It has only 78 pages, and most of them are lists, which we will skip.

> "A more serious mistake is the confusion between 𓏤 and 𓏤𓏤. The former of these letters is unquestionably an A, as proved by numerous transcriptions of proper names; as in Amon, Anubis, Alexandros. ... There are, however, cases in which, as in Coptic derivatives, 𓏤 even when initial is represented by an I." [*An Elementary Grammar of the Ancient Egyptian Language*, P. le Page Renouf, London, ca. 1874, p. viii].

The irony here is that the Anubis he cites as an example, ∤〰□⅋, should be read ⅋□〰∤ and not WPNI but rather MRNI, MORONI. The fact that ⅋ once carried the sounds M and W is preserved in the English alphabet, where W is the same letter as M, rotated 180 degrees. And that ∤ represents any vowel is represented by its cuneiform equivalent ⊏E which like ∤ usually represents I but can represent any vowel, the most frequent alternative being A as we see in ⊏E⟨, AD.

> "... we have no right to talk of an Egyptian alphabet, except as a device of modern scholars who, for their own purposes , have selected out of the phonetical signs of the Egyptians those most closely approximating in value to simple sounds. The Egyptians themselves knew of no alphabet; their signs, like those of all the older nations of antiquity, were expressive of *syllables*, and no syllabary can be pointed out from which the vowel sounds are absent. *Why should they?*"[op. cit., p. ix. Italics in original.]

Is he right? What is the difference between saying that ancient characters were written without vowels, and saying that they were actually syllables but that any vowel could either precede or follow the consonant? My researches indicate he was right, but that the rules of determining the vowels to precede or follow the consonant have not only been lost, but that the very need for the existence of any such rules has been obviated by the simplistic postulation of the existence of a writing system without vowels. Like the postulation of the existence of black holes to explain the phenomena of giant stars whose existence is not comprehended, so the postulation of a writing system without vowels is absurd. Egyptologists have complained of the absence of verbal tenses in the written language. Is this true? No more than the lack of tenses in Hebrew, wherein tenses are governed by vowels, not consonants, just as in English in the case of all our strong verbs, sing, sang, sung and the like. The key to all this is the knowledge of the existence of degrees and their rules of shifting. Both the Arabs and the Jews, once the knowledge of vowel shifting was lost, contrived a system of points to indicate what vowels went where. In the case of Arabic, the alternate consonant sounds borne by the original hieroglyphs are now indicated by points.

Now let's continue through Renouf's grammar, but making the necessary corrections. For simplicity, I am leaving off the determinatives, because we are concerned at this point only with the lexical part of the words. In the case of many nouns, just imagine a picture of the thing added after the hieroglyphs, which makes you wonder why the other hieroglyphs were needed.

Renouf has ∤◁◁〰\\ , IAANI, "ape." Our chart suggests IOHOHNI.

∤♁⟨🐦 , IUA, ox. I say ITUHA.

Continuing with Renouf, 1875:

⟨hieroglyphs⟩
AA ER TEFEF
Greater than his father.

⟨hieroglyphs⟩
NEFER ER SET HEMET NEBET
More beautiful than any other wife.

⟨hieroglyphs⟩
SHEPSES KHER SUTEN ER BAK NEB
Esteemed by the king more than any other servant.

⟨hieroglyphs⟩
MERERU HENEF ER BAKEF NEB
His majesty loved me more than any other servant of his.

More Early Egyptian

Now I want to show you something very interesting. I already demonstrated that the Egyptian quail chick hieroglyph, ⟨glyph⟩, should be read M, not W or U as claimed by Egyptologists. Remember, though, that we are talking about pre-Ptolemaic hieroglyphs. If this is the case, why is there another M sound with ⟨glyph⟩ which is said to be M? I left this alone in the chart because I didn't have time to make all the corrections and provide examples, without which the corrections would be questionable. The answer is, there are not two M hieroglyphs; ⟨glyph⟩ is not necessarily a superfluous M. It should sometimes be rendered B. But wait for more evidence of this.

Egyptologists say that the word for crocodile is ⟨glyphs⟩ and is pronounced EMSUH. I say, not in this case. ⟨glyph⟩ is here pronounced B. ⟨glyph⟩ in this instance is pronounced H. I already proved that ⟨glyph⟩ is M. And I already proved that in both Egyptian and Arabic, ⟨glyph⟩ at the end of a word can be pronounced TH. Do you see where this is taking us? ⟨glyphs⟩ is identical to the Hebrew בהמות which you recognize as BEHEMOTH. The word only occurs once in the Bible, in the book of Job, where Hebrew scholars suppose it refers to the hippopotamus, but it seems to have been used for any large or fearsome creature, including reptiles [see Gesenius, p. 96-7].

I already pointed out that ⟨glyphs⟩ which Egyptologists read as RETH should be read as LUTH, although the language actually permits it to be read both ways.

⟨glyphs⟩ should be read EPHEMERA not HRU; I said this much earlier but you see that it is the same as the Greek word of the same meaning, day.

Pharaoh

Ask any Egyptologist what the word Pharaoh means and he will tell you "great house." This is a false etymology which did not arise until a thousand years later, and the PER AA they map this word onto actually refers to the pharaoh's estate, not the pharaoh or any person at all.

Egyptologists will tell you that the oldest name for Egyptian rulers was ERPAT or ERPA (⬭◻⌐) and means hereditary king. This is partly right. The hieroglyphs should be read PHA RA OH and should be translated ⬭ (the hieroglyph called the mouth) as PHA = king, cognate with what Sumerologists call PA = the head, ruler, etc. as in PATESI. ⬭

The second hieroglyph ◻ that looks like a small square should be in this case rendered RA and means "royal." The third hieroglyph ⌐, the outstretched hand, forearm, and part of the arm, should be rendered OH and means "blood" in this instance. Thus, what is incorrectly read as ERPA(T) should be read PHA RA OH, "king by royal blood" (Abraham 1:20).

Life, Strength, Health

The three hieroglyphs that often follow the name of a pharaoh are said by Sir Alan Gardiner (Egyptian Grammar, p. 50) to mean "may he live, be prosperous, be healthy ... attributes bestowed on the king and on honored persons by the gods, and prayed for by men on their behalf; often appended as a token of respect to words for 'king', 'lord', etc." and are cited by other Egyptologists as "life, strength, health."

They are read backwards by every Egyptologist in the world and are not at all understood. This is another example of something of special significance being written in the opposite direction as the Egyptian way of doing what we do by way of capitalization. They are an indication that the pharaoh is at some future time to receive his endowment by the proper authority (which the Egyptians never had, notwithstanding they went through the motions anyway). The hieroglyph known to everyone as "ankh, meaning life" actually refers to the keys of the priesthood [which is why it is a representation of a key], again something the Egyptians never had, yet they imitated all the ordinances and recorded them anyway. The correct short-form expansion of the three hieroglyphs, which no Egyptologist does correctly, is "health, strength, priesthood" which will be immediately recognized by some individuals now that I have explained it. Even this brief expansion is in turn an abbreviation for a much longer text, which I will not repeat here nor anywhere else.

The Egyptian pharaonic epithet KA NHT "victorious bull" [Gardiner p.51] actually comes from Sumerian GUD MAH PA EH AH [exalted bull, glorious] which in turn comes from the language of Adam, AHMAN, which means "the Bull of Heaven" or in other words, the Bridegroom.

Aha or Menes

The first king of Egypt is generally called MENES but this is not his name. It is the Greek translation given by the Egyptian historian Manetho. He was named AHA and he was the grandson of Ham. AHA does not mean to stand or arise [Gardiner]. His name means "the abiding one" or "he who remains." That's why the name of the first king, AHA, became Μηνες (Menes) to the Greeks. He who remains. Meanings change over time. That was the original meaning. Josephus admits that the Greeks translated all proper nouns into their own language. He wrote:

> "After this they were dispersed abroad, on account of their languages, and went out by colonies everywhere; and each colony took possession of the land which they light upon, and unto which God led them; so that the whole continent was filled with them, both the inland and maritime countries. There were some also who passed over the sea in ships, and inhabited the islands; and some of those nations do still retain the denominations which were given them by their first founders; but some have lost them also; and some have only admitted certain changes in them, that they might be more intelligible to the inhabitants; and they were the Greeks who became the authors of such mutations; for when, in after ages, they grew potent, they claimed to themselves the glory of antiquity, -- giving names to the nations that sounded well (in Greek) that they might be better understood among themselves; and setting agreeable forms of government over them, as if they were a people derived from themselves." [Underlining added. Flavius Josephus, *Antiquities of the Jews*, ca. 100 A.D., translated from the Greek by William Whiston, Scotland, 1867, reprint by Kregel Publications, Grand Rapids, Michigan, fifth printing, 1967, Book I, Chapter V, p. 30. This little paragraph is the entire chapter.]

In the following chapter, he proceeds to give the Greek translation of the nations listed in Hebrew in Genesis 10.

This is why Manetho, writing in Greek, gives us Menes instead of Aha. But do you know why? That's okay, neither does anybody else. The answer is this: The Greeks had no choice. Their first writing system after the Tower of Babel was hieroglyphics: Linear B. Each one had a set of meanings. You could not write a sound without associating some meaning with it, whether you like it or not, exactly as Chinese today.

Psothom Phanech

Zaphnath-paaneah (Genesis 41:45) does not mean anything in any language. This is a scribal error. The correct transliteration is given by Josephus. Josephus wrote:

"Joseph was now grown up to thirty years of age, and enjoyed great honours from the king, who called him Psothom Phanech, out of regard to his prodigious degree of wisdom; for that name denotes *the revealer of secrets*." [Antiquities of the Jews Book II, Chapter 6, verse 1. Italics in original].

From his correct transliteration "Psothom Phanech" it is easy to translate the hieroglyphs as "the revealer of hidden things." In Josephus' Greek, this would be Ψοθομ Φανεχ.

Luther has Zaphenath-Paneach. The Masoretic Hebrew Bible has צפנת־פענח which should have been transliterated as Tsaphnath Pangnach. Nevertheless, these are all scribal errors and are all meaningless in any language. The Masoretic Hebrew Bible is known as the *Biblia Hebraica Stuttgartensia*, which is based upon the Leningrad Manuscript B19^A (L). "Auf jeden Fall ist L immer noch «die älteste datierte Handschrift der vollständigen hebräischen Bibel»." ["In any case, the L(eningrad codex) is 'the oldest dated manuscript of the complete Hebrew Bible.'"] The Leningrad codex is dated 1008 or 1009 A.D.

However, the Greek Septuagint has Ψοντομφανηχ [*Biblia Hebraica S.*, p. 63, apparatus. (An apparatus is a set of footnotes which list the textual variations found in other manuscripts.)] Note that this is practically identical to what Josephus cites - no surprise, since he is writing in Greek.
Now, the expression in Egyptian hieroglyphic for a secret, riddle, or something with a hidden meaning is ⟨hieroglyphs⟩ , pronounced ANEKH.

The expression for shedding light on a matter is ⟨hieroglyphs⟩ with an alternate reading in the so-called Book of the Dead as ⟨hieroglyphs⟩; both can be read as PSOTH; it carries both transitive and intransitive meanings of enlighten or to shine forth respectively. It is this expression that is inexplicably mistranslated by all scholars as "backbone" in the Book of the Dead. "Backbone" is ⟨hieroglyphs⟩ \, not

⟨hieroglyphs⟩. (The backslash should have five short perpendicular lines through it suggesting to the mind the backbone with its vertebrae, but that character is not provided in any of my fonts). In the Book of the Dead, this expression also occurs in the passage from the Book of Enoch that prophesies the coming of Lehi and Mulek to South and North America respectively (see http://www.72languages.com/hallofjudgment.php), but has been horribly mistranslated by every Egyptologist in the world. I will reproduce all the hieroglyphs here another day, but I have already given the traditional translation and the correct translation in a previous installment.

The final expression we need to know to translate this name is ⟨hieroglyphs⟩ with an alternate writing of ⟨hieroglyphs⟩. This denotes a person in authority. Any Egyptologist will tell you it is transliterated MR and this is true for Ptolemaic

Egyptian at the time of the Rosetta Stone, but in Joseph's day as I have already demonstrated repeatedly, it was equivalent to MUPH, ancestor of the Arabic word MUFTI, one who gives an authoritative or decisive response.

So the full Egyptian expression is 𓏏𓂝𓂧𓀀𓄿𓂝𓁐𓏺𓂻𓀀𓁐 and is pronounced PSOTHOMUPHANEKH which corresponds precisely with Josephus' Ψοθομ Φανεχ and means one who gives authoritative enlightenment on inscrutable matters.

The Tale of Two Brothers

The well-known Egyptian tale called The Tale of the Two Brothers is indeed a fairy tale the way it is translated. It is in fact the original Egyptian account of Joseph while in Potiphar's service when translated correctly. The hieroglyph for the servant |||| (four vertical lines), incorrectly read as Batau by some, the same "BIT" previously mentioned, is exactly the same as that in Joseph's pyramid, which should be translated Joseph. The hieroglyphs transliterated SEN AA and translated "elder brother" constitute an idiomatic expression precisely equivalent to the Chinese characters (Hsien Sheng or similar transliteration) of the same meaning, and are not to be translated "first born" but rather "master." Similarly, the Turkish ağabey (older brother) is often used to mean master as a term of respect. The characters transliterated SEN SERIU and translated "younger brother" constitute an analogous idiom and should be translated "servant." Many elements of the Joseph story are recognizable even in the tale's current translation, but a correct translation removes discrepancies and provides significant additional details.

Deseret

It is taught by all Egyptologists that there were two lands comprising Egypt, namely Upper [Southern] and Lower [Northern] Egypt, which were known respectively as the Black Land and the Red Land. Even the Hebrew name of Egypt, מצרים is a dual as everyone knows. These translations are basically correct but utterly incomplete and convey no information. Lower Egypt 𓇥 should be properly transliterated DESERET [not DSHRT] and Upper Egypt 𓈖, HAMET [not KMI] and mean respectively the Land of Joseph and the Land of Ham, or "the red land" and "the black land."

Champollion says that "le chef du peuple, le roi" is represented "par une espèce d'abeille 𓆤, parce que cet insecte est soumis à un gouvernement régulier." The defective reasoning would be excusable if it were the conjecture of why something is so, but if it were used to reach this conclusion, it is not excusable, because there are other insects, e.g. ants, which display more social order than bees, and even if bees were the most socially regulated, it would only make sense to have the queen bee denote royalty, yet even there the gender would be misleading.

Do you suppose later experts have figured out that 🐝 does not mean "king," or do you suppose they accepted Champollion's initial conjecture without question? Budge [An Egyptian Hieroglyphic Dictionary, Sir E. A. Wallis Budge, London, 1920, p.211] translates it BIT, "king of the north."

Gardiner [op. cit., p. 564] defines 🐝 as BIT, "bee" and as "king of lower Egypt."

Rainer Hannig does not include 🐝 alone in his dictionary at all but lists 🐝⌐ as "BJT, Biene; das unterägyptischen (nordägyptischen) Königtum" [BIT, bee; the lower Egyptian (north Egyptian) kingdom,"] [*Die Sprache der Pharaonen: Großes Handwörterbuch Ägyptisch-Deutsch* (2800-950 v. Chr.), Verlag Philipp von Zabern, Mainz, 1995, p. 245].

Adolf Erman, widely acknowledged the greatest Egyptian lexicographer of them all, has only 🐝⌐, not 🐝 alone, and he says: "BJT, die Biene: I. als wirkliches Tier I. II. Bes. als Sinnbild des unterägyptischen Königtums ... So auch in dem Titel des ägyptischen Königs..." [p. 412, *Wörterbuch der AEgyptischen Sprache*, Akademie Verlag, Berlin, 1971, vol. 1].

🐝 does not refer to a king at all but to a land except in the first degree, where, as Erman says, it is used "as the actual animal." It should in the other degrees be translated as the Land of Joseph, the Western Land, the Holy Land, and the Red Land. With this corrected and expanded translation it makes perfect sense in every instance where it is used, as part of the king's title: "the king of the Black Land [upper Egypt] and of the Red Land [lower Egypt]."

The BIT transliteration of 🐝 is erroneous; it comes from the fourth hieroglyph in Joseph's tomb, ||||, which is also transliterated erroneously "BIT." The reason for this error is that the latter hieroglyph, which also occurs in Sumerian as ⊨𝍩, likewise misread BIT because it is related to BETH, abode. In all these instances it should be read JOSEPH.

The hieroglyphic spelling of 🐝 is 🦆⚊⬭⌐ . This is 🐝 spelled out. It is also spelled ⬭⚊⬭⌐🦆 by Egyptologists but a more accurate spelling would be 🦆⬭⚊⬭⌐ . Any of the first three characters is often left out because it was obvious to the Egyptians. Here is the correct transliteration and translation of 🐝 straight from the Egyptians themselves:

🦆 DE, find. Usually transliterated QEM by Egyptologists.

⬭ , an optional phonetic compliment DE showing how 🦆 should be pronounced in this instance.

▥▥▥, often simplified to merely ▭, pronounced S in this case. This denotes a rock with water in it, thereby signifying *pure* water. This hieroglyph was shown to the Israelites in the wilderness out of Egypt (Numbers 20:8-11), and also to John in his vision of the Savior's throne (Revelation 22:1). This same hieroglyph is shown under the throne of Jehovah in Abraham's Egyptian description of the Bar of Judgment, where it denotes the pure gospel flowing out from the foundation of the Savior's throne to the four quarters of the earth (see http://72languages.com/hallofjudgment.php). In other words, the pure gospel issuing forth from the cavity of a rock, ▥♈⤝⎺, BUR NA, which also denotes humility. Some will recognize in this also the origin of the "book seen by three/eight witnesses" mentioned in the Bar of Judgment, which also issued forth from the cavity of a rock.

The hieroglyph ⌒ in this instance is simply the preposition "for" and pronounced R is the ancestor of that word in all Western European languages, and in Semitic languages in its capacity to represent the L sound and in the Finno-Ugric languages as a suffix of the same meaning in its capacity to represent the R sound (see prior discussion of the Egyptian R-L transformation).

The final hieroglyph ⌒, denotes seed, grain or bread; also land, and a feminine suffix pronounced –T or -ET. Sometimes it is affixed also to the 𓆤 but in that instance it is a signific compliment indicating that a land is signified.

So this etymology of the fully spelled out Egyptian expression takes us back to the original language of Adam: "𓅱 find - ▥▥▥ pure water - ⌒ for - ⌒ seeds or bread," - a function of the honeybee known to the Jaredites, and pronounced DESERET.

With the simultaneous capacity for the 𓅱 D hieroglyph to soften to J and the ⌒ R hieroglyph to harden to PH, we have the "land of Joseph." The hieroglyph of the honey bee 𓆤 should be read Joseph in its soft form, and when followed by the hieroglyph ⌒ (sound T) should then be read in its hard form, Deseret. Many modern languages also experience a pattern of consonants having both soft and hard sounds, the expression of which depends upon grammatical rules.

Egyptologists have been haggling about SUTEN-BIT or NESUBIT as the proper pronunciation for the hieroglyphs for the king of Egypt. They are all wrong. BIT |||| (four vertical lines) is the same as it is in "Zoser's" tomb - Joseph. It may be translated as "king of the Holy Land" as I explained earlier, Deseret. Certainly Brigham must have heard it from Joseph Smith. Deseret is the proper name of North and South America in the language of Adam. The name of the hieroglyph is the honeybee, as mentioned by Joseph Smith in the first place. Even before the continental shift, it was the Western Land as it is today.

Egyptian Hieroglyphic and Chinese

I want to show an example vindicating Samuel Birch's belief that knowledge of Chinese is essential to an understanding of Egyptian Hieroglyphic.

In the Book of the Dead, page 22 [plate V, BD chapter I] we have:

Now, this is a very interesting statement because it reveals and proves a lot of things.

First, here is Budge's transliteration:
NUK UR KHERP AB HRU ERDAT HENNU SEKER HER MAKHAIT TUF
[I have replaced X by KH which is how it was intended to be pronounced, etc.]

Why does Budge ignore the ⟨⟩ ? It has a well documented M sound, usually MR although the Egyptians were known to suppress a final R sound to an AH like our own Southern or Massachusetts dialects. In fact, the Joseph Smith Grammar and Alphabet of the Egyptian Language documents that the Egyptians treated the R exactly like today's Bostonians: FAR was pronounced FAH and AH was pronounced AR. Remember JFK's FAH for FAR and IDEAR for IDEA? The JS GAEL has instances of ELKENER for ELKENAH as an example, but the official version retained is the latter form.

This is an important question, because HENNU has an entirely different meaning from HEMENNU which is the correct reading. The former means "within" and the latter means "eight." These facts are thoroughly documented by any and all Egyptian dictionaries and grammars.

Budge's translation is: "I am the great chief of the work on the day of placing the hennu boat of Seker upon its sledge."

Faulkner's translation, "acknowledged as the finest English translation of the text" [The Egyptian Book of the Dead, tr. Dr. Raymond Faulkner, 1998, Chronicle Books, back cover] is in no material way better: "I am the Master Craftsman on the day of placing the Bark of Sokar on its sledge." [plate 5 right, op. cit.].

In fact, Budge's translation is better. "great chief of the work" is a better translation than "Master Craftsman." The operation does not involve craftsmanship; it involves project management.

The key word here is the hennu boat, which Budge transliterates almost correctly, leaving out the M, but Faulkner altogether ignores!

It is the HEMENNU boat, the "boat of the Eight," an expression for Noah's Ark which bore the body of Adam.

In fact, the MAKHAIT which is translated both by Budge and Faulkner as sledge, is followed by a character which both Budge and Faulkner ignore presumably on the grounds that it is a determinative: ⟦𓊨𓊨𓊨⟧. But ⟦𓊨𓊨𓊨⟧ is the hieroglyph for ADAM, misread TEM by Egyptologists. Nibley knew that it should be read ADAM.

It is not incorrect to read 𓄿 ⟶ 𓏏 𓄿 𓏭𓏭 𓊨𓊨𓊨 as sledge, but it is incomplete. The full meaning is "the carrier of Adam." MAKHAIT, you may recall, is the word for "scales" or "balance" in the Bar of Judgment; here it is "sledge." It is simply a generic term for something that carries or supports something.
2765. The correct translation of

𓂋𓄿𓃀𓃀𓂋𓏏𓏏𓄿𓉐𓂋𓅡𓇳𓇳𓂋𓏏𓃀𓅓𓊪𓂋𓅡𓂋𓃀𓇳𓏭𓊨𓊨𓊨: 𓇯𓄿𓂋

𓏏𓄿𓏭𓏭𓊨𓊨𓊨𓂋𓅡𓆑

is "I am the project manager of the work on the day of placing the Vessel of Eight [Ark of Noah] used for transporting the body of Adam, upon its sledge."

SKR, rendered SEKER by Budge and SOKAR by Faulkner, is not a person at all; there is no determinative of a person or god in the original text. It means to transport by boat, for which there **is** a determinative in the original text.

Faulkner once again here merely rewords slightly or echoes word for word, Budge. If Budge is discredited to the point that anyone who even quotes him as an authority on anything is himself discredited, as claimed recently by an Egyptologist, what is to become of Faulkner?

Another key expression that Faulkner copies from Budge word for word is 𓉐𓂋𓅡𓇳𓏭𓂋𓏏𓄿, "on the day of placing." This translation is correct, but its significance seems to be lost on everybody. Why would the Egyptians place Noah's Ark on a sledge and drag it through the streets on a special day? For the same reason the ancient German tribes cut down a tree [Tannenbaum] of the wood the Ark was made of [Tannenholz] and brought it into the house and adorned it as a symbol of life being supported by this tree at a time when all the rest of the world was buried under a shroud of water [in the form of snow in the Germans' case].

This day for the Egyptians would be 10 May, in commemoration of 10 May 2197 B.C., the day Noah entered the Ark.

Now the word in Chinese for a boat, vessel, or ship, is 船, CHUAN. Shall we analyze this character?

The radical on the left, 肉 is radical Nº130, flesh, meat, body; the combining form is identical to radical Nº74, 月 moon or month. The Egyptian original is 𓄹 ; the cuneiform original is ⸢corpse⸣, corpse, blood, die, which in turn is cognate with ⸢blood⸣, blood.

八 is the number 8. It also carries the idea of division.

口 . This is identical in form and meaning to the old cuneiform ⸢cuneiform⸣. The three horizontal lines to the left are merely an augmentative. The Chinese character came from this cuneiform as a single radical but was split into its separate meanings for radical Nº30 as the great opening, i.e. the mouth, and radical Nº31 as the great enclosure. The original character simultaneously served the notion of keeping things out [the great opening as in digging a hole by removing dirt out of it, or the walls of a city or fortress] and keeping things in, as a vessel or walls of a prison.

So, 船 means a divided vessel of eight [persons] carrying also a dead body. Of course, four thousand years later, the individual components are forgotten and only the meaning of vessel is retained in Chinese.

Divided? In the Ark, all males were housed on the right side of the beam, and all females, man and beast alike, were housed on the left side of the beam. Some religious performances retain this observance to this day. In the Ark, this prevented cohabitation, which would have complicated things a great deal, as you can imagine.

I hope you have been able to infer from such data what kind of shape modern Egyptology is in. I hope you can see why all Egyptian records, especially the older ones, need to be retranslated. For over a hundred hears, Egyptologists have been cowpathing, i.e. mindlessly parroting the work of their predecessors and not only failing to correct their errors, but actually not doing as well as their mentors. Everybody I ever heard criticize Nibley seemed to be motivated by sheer jealousy. My only criticism of him was that he was wrong about some major things such as the Jaredites not retaining the original language and the sen-sen papyrii not being the source of the Book of Abraham. But so what? All the other scholars are wrong about this latter, most important point too. I don't see Nibley's equal anywhere on the horizon.

Paut Khemenu

This is called by scholars the Paut Khemenu, the Company of the Eight, and is supposed to be the eight primeval gods of the Creation. Their transliterations are given beside each character. Back in 1987 I discovered that the so-called "Paut Khemenu" or Company of the Eight is in fact Noah and his family.

Let's start with a set of hieroglyphs very familiar to Egyptologists.

Now, you can take this little list of hieroglyphs to any Egyptologist in the world and he will tell you that:

This is the so-called Paut Khemennu, or Company of the Eight.

These are the primeval gods of Egypt.

Their names are Nu, Nut, Keku, Kekut, Gerekh, Gerekhet, Hehu and Hehut.

Doesn't that send a thrill down your spine, to be privy to this exciting and inspiring information and insight?

These hieroglyphs are in the oldest form of Egyptian, which is also the language of Adam.

Each hieroglyph has several sounds, and each sound has its own meaning or meanings.

This is the ship's register of the crew and passengers (human passengers) on Noah's Ark.

The ⌒ hieroglyph is transcribed T as any Egyptologist knows and is a sign of the feminine. So each name in the right column may be translated the same as the name in the left column, with the prefix "Mrs." in front of it.

Remember in Hindustani we saw that each letter that performed some function had an equivalent analog in English [and every other language] performing the same function? For example, the interrogative KA in Hindustani and Japanese performs the same function as MA in Chinese and Hebrew and W in English [where, what, who, why, when, etc.].

Okay, now let's construct a chart - remember I did this before and called it The Foundation of Egyptology because it can be used to overhaul the field and produce correct translations. I also told you the first time I posted it that it was not complete and that I would complete it later as time permits.

Nu they got right, although they do not recognize it as Noah. It is preserved in Persian as Nuh, their word for Noah. Ararat, for example, is called in Persian "Kuh Nuh" - the Mountain of Noah. Nut is Noah's wife. All the hieroglyphs at the right are the female counterparts (wives) with the feminine suffix -t.

We're going to skip Noah. You already know that his name means "respite." You can also see that it is obvious enough that we don't have to say anything more about it. The Persians still call Noah "Nuh."

Ham, Shem, and Japheth

Egyptologists call these KEKU, HEHU, and GEREKH respectively as part of the "Paut Khemennu" or "Company of the Eight," which tells you and me exactly nothing.

The two flax twines to the right of HEHU are rendered by scholars as H - H. This is correct at the beginning of a word.

The quail chick to the right of the two twines is rendered by all Egyptologists as U or W. It should be rendered M. Anciently the W and M were rotated to express which sound was intended. The correct reading of this hieroglyph is HAM, not HEHU. The Egyptians listed Ham first, even though he was not the oldest son, because he was their ancestor.

The two shallow baskets to the right of KEKUI with the little loop handles on the right are rendered by all the scholars in the world as K. They should be rendered SH as the doubled SHIN in Hebrew. The quail chick again should be rendered as M. The correct reading of this hieroglyph is SHEM, not KEKUI.

What is rendered KEREH with a dot under the K is deceiving. Even scholars know that the K with a dot under it is the sound for G. But the little stool with the triangle under it should be rendered as a softened G as in George, or more correctly J. The pointed oval that looks like an opening and closing parenthesis turned on its side, is rendered by all scholars in the world as R. It should be rendered Ph. It is the ancestor, through Phoenician, of the Greek P (rho) which is pronounced as our R, and the Roman P which is pronounced like our P. The final flax twine in KEREH is rendered by all scholars in the world as H. This is correct at the beginning and medial positions of a word, but in the final position of a word it is used exactly like its Arabic descendant, which is Th. So this final hieroglyph should be rendered JAPHETH and not KEREH or GEREH.

The boat is of course the Ark, and the "primeval watery abyss of NU" is the Flood. The whole set of hieroglyphs is not a representation of the Egyptian notion of the Creation, but a simple and obvious representation of the Flood. The hieroglyph of the beetle represents the body of Adam carried aboard the Ark. Although these eight hieroglyphs are commonly represented as being aboard a boat, the scholars still do not get it. Is it any wonder than ancient language is so boring with the way they translate things?

Hieroglyph	Traditional value accepted by Egyptologists -i.e. the values at the time of the Rosetta Stone, 198 B.C.	Values which must be known and used in order to translate correctly Egyptian hieroglyphic much earlier than Ptolemaic Egyptian
⟨bowl⟩	K	SH, H
⟨bird⟩	W	M, B
⟨flax twine⟩	H	H, K, S, TH,
⟨stool⟩	G	G, J, O
⟨oval⟩	R, L	PH, L, M

Now we get ⟨glyphs⟩ = SHEM.

And we get ⟨glyphs⟩ = JAPHETH.

And we get 𓏲𓏲𓅨 = HAM.

Is this a bit more enlightening? This has brought us up to the level of English. We know their names.

Now let's extract the full value contained in the language of Adam.

Just as SHU can be read USHU, so also SHEM can be read SHEMESH. This is convenient, because we know from Hebrew that שמש SHEMESH means "sun."

But we also find 𓂝𓂝𓅨 written 𓂝𓅨𓂝, so that we can also read it SHINEHAH, which is the language of Adam word for "sun."

An additional reading of 𓊖𓂝𓏲 is OLEAH which is the language of Adam word for "moon."

An additional reading for 𓏲𓏲𓅨 is KOKOB which is the Adamic word for "star." It is also preserved in Hebrew as כוכב which also happens to be transliterated KOKOB.

These three names are given by way of representation of the glory to be inherited if they keep their respective covenants, as explained in an earlier installment.

But there's more. SHEM can also be read MESH as it is incorrectly by scholars in GILGAMESH. [In that instance it is written backwards by way of "capitalization" by way of a proper noun and should be read "Shem."]. But MESH needs to be considered here in its own right; it is the Adamic word for "birth," preserved in Egyptian as 𓄟, MESH, birth.

𓊖𓂝𓏲 can also be read as GAMOS which is the language of Adam word for "marriage," which the Greeks have preserved for us as γαμος, GAMOS, "marriage."

All syllables in the original language can be read in either direction as we have already demonstrated previously as well as here.

𓏲𓏲𓅨 can also be read MUTH which is the Adamic word for "death."

The language of Adam is highly elliptical, as we saw with the writing on Belshazzar's wall. Here in this case we have the three covenants of the respective posterities of Shem, Japheth, and Ham:

Shem: I will keep the law of chastity from birth, for which I will inherit a kingdom whose glory is like unto the sun.

Japheth: I will keep the law of chastity from marriage, for which I will inherit a kingdom whose glory is like unto the moon.

Ham: I will be responsible for my own sins until death and do no murder [willfully cause the death of any innocent person], for which I will inherit a kingdom whose glory is like unto the stars.

Of course, anyone is free to live by a higher or lower covenant, as Jesus illustrated in the parable of the father asking his two sons to work in the field.

With further translation, we see the standing of each individual in the eternal family according to which covenant he actually lives up to:

SHEM is the Adamic word for "son." This is preserved in Danish surnames as the suffix -sen .

GEREKH is the Adamic word for "stranger, foreigner" preserved in Hebrew גרח GEREKH, stranger, foreigner.

HAM is the Adamic word for negro and "servant." Ham's mother was a negress, as was his wife. This is why the Scriptures go to the trouble to point out that Shem was born of the same mother as Japheth.

None of this should be construed as any pretext or justification for racial bigotry. These are nothing more than covenants under which we are born into the Second Estate. All that matters once we are here is what covenant we actually live up to. There is no respect of persons at the Bar of Judgment and every person has an equal chance to rise or fall entirely by his own will.

Japheth also means "healed" but I think we have shown enough to give you sufficient understanding as to how the language of Adam works.

Exactly what happened at the Tower of Babel so that each nation walked away with a completely intact language that was completely incomprehensible to every other nation?

Every nation got only one sound and forgot the others. Thus, to the Greeks, ▣�buttonmeant "marriage." To the Hebrews it meant "stranger." To another nation it meant "moon," and so on.

For example, in the language of Adam, ⌣ PHA means "king" in the highest degree. In the first degree it simply means "mouth." The Slavs got the R sound, so their word for "mouth" is рто, RTO or ROT. The Germanic tribes got the M sound, so our word for MOUTH is the same but with the R converted to an M.

The example in the foregoing entry also meant "red" so ROT[H] in German also means "red," and so on.

Now you know exactly what happened at the Tower of Babel. And you see why we can, if we know exactly what happened, reverse engineer the language of Adam if we know the 70 languages into which it was prismatically divided and work out the obvious transforms.

Shem: ⌣ ⌣ 𓅓 𓆓

Sun, son, birth. This is preserved in the Babylonian 𒈠𒌋 SHAMASH, sun, and the Egyptian 𓄟 MESH, birth (remember that words in the original language could be read forwards or backwards), and is the ancestor of later words including Anglo-Saxon sunu = son, and sunnu = sun (The SH-S transformation and M-N transformations seen in transitions between many languages are discussed here: http://72languages.com/originallanguage.php).

There is reason to suspect that Hammurabi (Hammu=priest; Rabi= augmentative, high) was a title of Shem, the great high priest (D&C 138:41) [as was also Melchizedek, "King of Righteousness."] We know historically that the people of Shem were essentially in a state of civil war until he devised a civil code that brought peace and order to his people.

Japheth: ⌂ ⬡ 𓏏𓏏𓅱
Stranger or foreigner, healing or marriage, moon. More obvious in its Egyptian form GEREKH which is preserved as the Hebrew word גרה for "stranger" or "foreigner." An alternate reading is Oleah, an old word for the moon. Hebraists generally cite יפה Jafa, "the fair one" which is an allusion to the moon. Given the Egyptian L<-->R/P transformation and the transition of H to TH at the end of a word as still preserved in modern Arabic, it is easy to see that JAPHETH and OLEAH/OLAHA are the same word. In fact, it is by running through these transforms that all the meanings of a word in the language of Adam are extracted: OLAHA=moon, JAPHETH=the fair one; GEREKH=stranger, foreigner.

Ham: 𓏏𓏏𓆓𓅱
Servant, death, star. Preserved in the Hebrew מוות Maveth (death), Egyptian Ham 𓏏𓅦 (servant), etc.

The layman may find evidence that Sun, Moon, and Star are correct translations from the fact that the previously cited Paut Khemmenu was thought to be the Egyptian mythology of the Creation because it mentioned the Sun, Moon, and Stars, which are in fact correct partial translations of these names, as already mentioned.

A complete translation of these names as understood by the ancients would indicate that the posterity of Shem were born in a covenant by which they would keep the law of chastity from birth and thereby receive an inheritance in a kingdom compared to the sun. Japheth in full translation indicates a covenant by which they would keep the law of chastity from marriage and thereby receive an inheritance in a kingdom compared to the moon. Ham in full translation indicates a covenant by which they would do no murder (death) and be responsible for their own sins until death, by which they would receive at least an inheritance in a kingdom compared to the stars. Note that these covenants are alluded to in the New Testament: "now ye are no longer strangers and foreigners ..." and that it is made perfectly clear that what really matters is not what a man has covenanted that he would do, but what law he actually chooses to live by once he gets here (cf. the parable of the two sons being asked to go labor in the field, Matthew 21:28-32).

It will now become evident to a thoughtful person that the token of the house of Shem is gold, representing the morning aurora heralding the birth of the sun. Likewise, the token of the house of Japheth is frankincense, a healing balm. By now the reader can fill in the third part and final part of the pattern with the embalming myrrh as the token of the house of Ham.

Moroni

This person is represented in hieroglyphs by what is called by Egyptologists as INPU, although they generally cite the Greek form of the word, Anubis. However, this is a proper noun, and by way of respect is written in the opposite direction. The quail chick ⟨glyph⟩ rendered U should be rendered M as demonstrated earlier, and the square box hieroglyph ⟨glyph⟩ rendered P should be rendered R, also as already demonstrated. The correct reading is MRNI, or more completely, MORONI.

The Sphinx

Who built the sphinx? I have not as yet been able to find anyone who knows. It was built by the grandson of Ham, the first pharaoh, Aha, called by Manetho, Menes, which is nothing more than a translation into Greek of the Egyptian word Aha.

When was the sphinx built? About 1695 B.C.

Why was the sphinx built? As a tribute to Shem, or Melchizedek, Aha's great uncle.

What is the significance of the sphinx? It is a three dimensional hieroglyph. Translated, it means "man of holiness."

Moses

Ask any Egyptologist you want how the name Moses was written in the word's native language. If he is honest, he will tell you that he does not know. He may even go so far as to say that no one knows, which is almost correct. What everybody does know is that it means "delivered from the water" or "redeemed from the water" because Josephus said so ("the Egyptians call water by the name of Mo, and such as are saved out of it, by the name of Uses: so by putting these two words together, they imposed this name upon him" – Antiquities of the Jews book 2 chapter 9 v. 6), but now you will recognize it when you see it in the hieroglyphs.

The word Moses is not Hebrew, but the Hebrew transliteration of it is משה, MOSHEH. It isn't really possible to write MUISIS in Hebrew, or it wasn't in 1480 B.C. when Moses was born. When you attempt to write it - remember Hebrew has no vowels - you get מש or מששׁ, neither of which conveys unambiguously the idea of MUISIS. The correct writing is משה but when you double the letter שׁ [SHIN] it is now pronounced as an SH, so you get MOSHEH.

The correct original writing and etymology of the name Moses is written with two Egyptian hieroglyphs - the three wavy lines 〰 representing "water" and pronounced "MU" written over the single hieroglyph for Isis (𝕝), MU-ISIS: 〰𝕝. It is

read 〰 MU 𝕝 IS IS and means "water-delivered," "water-borne," or "water-redeemed."

Oliblish

Can anyone translate Oliblish? Who, other than Joseph Smith? Would you like me to translate Oliblish for you? The word LIB [also, RUB – see the Egyptian R/L transformation above] means "heart" or "center" and is the same root as in "cheRUB," [Hebrew כרוב , "warrior within," warrior class of angel, Arabic كرب, KHARB, "war"]. Now you can translate it. It is in the language of Adam. It is also correct to call it Egyptian at the time of Abraham. The first character in the word is 𝞱. It is the same 𝞱 that occurs as TU in ⬭𝞱🦅⚬ DAH TU HAH DEES and as O in the name of the Jaredite king, Omer. And it has the same meaning. "Remote [to any extent, even merely separate] in time and space." It also can mean "downward." In this case it means merely "downward" and "separate from," as the Greek roots έταιρ, έταρ, έτερ mean "companion," and "different," respectively, the ancestor of the Latin "etc." "et ca etera" [the "etera" being the ancestor of our "other"] which does not mean "and so on" [although the Russian equivalent, "итд.," "и так далее" [literally, "and so further"] means exactly that. In this case the 𝞱 pronounced "O" means precisely the same as the three Greek roots [which are really all the same root, and which we borrow in the same form "hetero-"] and it means "separate, different, companion" and does not carry the connotation of "remote." So what does OLIBLISH mean? Remember that LISH is the second character in the name of God in the language of Adam. It means council, intelligence, glory, etc. OLIBLISH means "separate from, downward from, but yet a companion to the heart [center] of glory" -- in other words from the giant star FLOS ISIS. This second governing star is the closest one to FLOS ISIS, which you remember means "light-mother," the giant star hidden behind the horsehead nebula in the constellation of Orion. Downward? Isn't any direction from heaven downward?

Zenos and Zenoch

Zenos and Zenock were in Egypt, after Joseph but before Moses. They were both - you may insert some small ordinal number here - great grandsons of Joseph. How do I know? 3 Nephi 10:16. I found both their names in Egyptian hieroglyphics. Both of their books still exist, and they are in hieroglyphics, but they are not as yet even recognized by any scholar I am aware of, much less translated correctly.

⸻ (hieroglyphs) is the hieroglyphic name of the prophet Zenock, a great grandson of Joseph, who was stoned by the Israelites, thus postponing their freedom from bondage until the days of Moses.

One spelling of the name Zenos appears in hieroglyphs as ⸻ (hieroglyphs) illustrating the Z soft sound of ⸻ as opposed to its more usual D sound we find in Ptolemaic Egyptian. This is preserved in ancient Venetic for example in an inscription on a tool found in northeastern Italy: "Mexo Vhuxiia zonasto Rehtiiah" ["I was presented by Vhuxia to Rehtia"] where the Italic verb "donare" with the Hellenic Aorist-like suffix -sto" has assumed the softened pronunciation (Z) in the Venetic branch, "zonasto." [See Johannes Friedrich, *Entzifferung Verschollener Schriften und Sprachen*, trans. by Frank Gaynor as *Extinct Languages*, 1957, p. 145].

Set
The so-called "Set" or "Seth" as called by Egyptologists should be read "Satan." I do not know why they persist in ignoring the final N which is given in some of the hieroglyphs - perhaps because it seems to be left off in some spellings of his name. The sixteen parts into which the body of Osiris was said by the Egyptians to been divided by "Set" are a representation of the sixteen grandsons of Noah into which the world's population was divided in the first generation after the Flood. ("The sons of Japheth; Gomer, and Magog, and Madai, and Javan, and Tubal, and Meshech, and Tiras...And the sons of Ham; Cush, and Mizraim, and Phut, and Canaan...The children of Shem; Elam, and Asshur, and Arphaxad, and Lud, and Aram." [Genesis 10: 2,6,22])

Book of Jasher
The so-called "Book of Aker" inscribed on the north wall of the tomb of Ramses VI in the Valley of the Kings at Thebes seems to be the missing "Book of Jasher" mentioned in the Old Testament. It has long been known that the translation of the Hebrew manuscript in the British Museum is not very good, but the Egyptian version has no good translation at all.

Miscellaneous
Genesis 21:30 " ...I have digged this well." Independent Egyptian records, which we shall examine in future installments, state that Abraham had developed technology to determine the presence of water deep underground.

The Sen-Sen Papyrus
It appears that the sen-sen papyrus from which the Book of Abraham was partially translated was on the mummified body of princess Katumin, daughter of Pharoah Onitas. The Joseph Smith Grammar and Alphabet of the Egyptian Language (JS GAEL) records: "Katumin, Princess, daughter of On-i-tos Pharoah – King of Egypt, who began to reign in the year of the world 2962. Katumin was born in the 30th year of the reign of her father, and died when she was 28 years

old, which was the year 3020." The paragraph describing the birth and death of Katumin written outside the scroll accompanying the body can only refer to the body it was placed on. These scrolls were as a rule placed on the breast of the embalmed body.

Late Egyptian Numbers

Here is the numeral 1: | Same as Chinese and Roman, and used in the same way: Two is || , and so on up through 9. 10 is ∩. 100 is ℮ . 1000 is ⚱ . 10,000 is a finger, ⎰. 100,000 is ⍦. 1,000,000 is ⍨ .

All these signs are from late Egyptian. Originally, there were ten separate, simple hieroglyphs for the numbers 1-10. In fact all our "Arabic" digits are from ancient Egypt, through Arabia, India, and then back to Egypt where they originated. I have no font for the original digits, but suffice it to say that they looked much like Arabic and Sanskrit characters.

Fractions were derived from the eye hieroglyph. Not the simple one ⬭ but the fancy one ⍻. The left triangle ◁ represented ½. The pupil ○ was ¼. The eyebrow ⌒ was 1/8. The triangle on the right ▷ was 1/16. The curved line ⌡ was 1/32. The vertical line was 1/64.

Printed in Great Britain
by Amazon

28579415R00037